LEWIS
BALTZ
TEXTS

LEWIS BALTZ TEXTS

Introduction by
Matthew S. Witkovsky

STEIDL

This book is for Elliot Ruchowitz-Roberts

Table of Contents

September 12, 2011

Lewis Baltz was formed in a generation of artist-critics. The seismic change in American art around 1960 was discursive as much as visual; after two decades in which artists sought at all costs to deny reference to their peers, the adherents of Minimal and post-Minimal art debated and built mightily upon one another's work. It is impossible to understand Carl Andre's cedar blocks without addressing his M.A. thesis on Constantin Brancusi or his dialogues with filmmaker Hollis Frampton, himself a practiced essayist on subjects in film and photography.[1] Essays and reviews by Allan Kaprow, Donald Judd, and later Robert Morris or Mel Bochner, were all likewise essential to the development of their work, and a certain strain of Anglo-American Conceptual Art became outright "bookish" in response to those critical debates.

Artists intent on revitalizing the possibilities of photography, such as Martha Rosler, Allan Sekula, or Victor Burgin made revisionist scholarship an especially strong part of their creative career; "theoreticians who also practice," as Baltz wrote in a 1995 essay on Sekula included in this anthology. One might expect Baltz to match that approach in the writings gathered here, especially as Rosler and Sekula were living and working in southern California in the early 1970s, along with other stern photographic laborers such as Fred Lonidier. But Baltz, for all his acerbic acumen, is no moralist. Noting in that essay the battle that raged between Sekula and mainstream curators at that time, "forceful in their moment," he states of Sekula's adversaries (MoMA, Eastman House) their fall from grace is now so complete that many of Sekula's texts read like "dispatches from a victorious but distant and half-forgotten war."

Unlike his erstwhile California colleagues, Baltz was writing after the fact, and he did not start practicing criticism regurarly until he was several years removed from his artistic and intellectual origins – all but six of the essays here were written for European audiences. The concision of Baltz's formulations is impossible to separate from his vantage of a more mature artist and an expatriate (Baltz moved abroad permanently i n 1985). This very distance is also what makes the essays fascinating to read today, and guarantees their interest for years to come. Baltz the writer is not "in the trenches," but he is very much attentive to important artists and debates, whether these touch directly on his art or not. The breadth of his interests, running from cinema to opera to urban planning and immigration rights, is refreshing, as is his determination not to confuse criticism with artistic self-legitimation.

For an American reader, the topics and tone of these mostly short pieces are alternately familiar and surprising, the result of Baltz's hybrid roots in either side of the Atlantic Ocean. Few native English writers, let alone an artist so utterly identified with the prefab desert landscape of postwar southern California, would think to begin an essay with the line, "There's a story in Zurich that refuses to die…"; the title to that essay, "Learning from Luxembourg," nevertheless gives such intellectual hybridity a knowing ring that makes it almost natural to accept. The caustic distillations that pepper these essays remind one of an earlier generation of feuilleton writers, on the order of H. L. Mencken or Karl Kraus: newspaper essayists battling the dumb prose of the daily newspaper. That battle can lead to cynicism and despair, but those traits happily do not come through here. Instead, we have a clear picture of Baltz the educator, wishing to place his expert insights at the service of a broad readership. Here he is in 1988, meditating presciently on the fate of Europe's most important contemporary city:

London, Paris, Rome, have a history, but Berlin has a past. It is the Sodom of our century, destroyed for its sins and left like that as a dark memorial. Since the 1920s, Berlin has been a city approached through images: Döblin, Pabst, Isherwood; the vicious shrine of Nazism; the Zero Hour; the Airlift, John Kennedy and the spies who came in from the cold; the generation of 68, the stylized desperation of the punk underground and angels you can touch, these are some of the images making the myth. Myths, however, do not only lend events a human dimension, they are also manufactured to mystify experiences. Mythic images are perhaps those you have to be most suspicious of. Yet the idea of a post-apocalyptic city captivates the contemporary spirit and images of it spring like mushrooms again. Berlin will soon be as flooded with pictures as New York and Paris and the images of the city will have lost all their power, except to reflect on and to remind one of each other.

One notes first Baltz's courage, as an American and a writer outside of expert literary-historical circles, to tackle a capacious summation of Berlin's historical significance; then one admires his ambition to make that summation as a means of drawing a general audience into a far narrower discussion of photographer Michael Schmidt and recent developments in the fine arts. Baltz goes from the general to the specific and expert, but also brings work out of a field of expertise (art, photography) to meet the broader world. He retains in his writing that utopian impulse characteristic of the best avant-gardes to "use" art – make it, exhibit it, reflect on it – as a means of understanding momentous historical shifts, and he does this insightfully and unpretentiously.

One of the best essays in this volume is nevertheless solidly on American photography, Baltz's expert domain. "Too Old to Rock, Too Young to Die," its too-catchy title notwithstanding, is the earliest (1985) and still in many ways the most trenchant overview yet written on American photography of the 1960s and '70s, Baltz's formative years. Here too, Baltz begins by charting history through images, offering wittily that the 1970s seem a far better decade if you follow the line that leads from Diane Arbus to Cindy Sherman rather than the one that runs from the Kent State killings to the election of Ronald Reagan. Photography boomed in the 1970s, for reasons that Baltz finds intriguing yet largely superficial. Perhaps it was simply a cyclical fashion, as he reports Castelli Graphics director Marvin Heiferman saying; perhaps it was merely an opportunity brought by exhaustion in more established areas of visual art. Fundamentally, as Baltz asserts with caustic insight, photography succeeded because the American art audience hankers for recognizable, anecdotal images, pictures that tell a story: "Thus," he concludes, "photography inherited some of that portion of the American art audience too intellectually torpid to understand, much less take interest in, the kinds of issues raised by the best American art of the 1960s."

This is a fabulous comment, not dismissive but disappointed; and Baltz's ability to see that limitation, as well as to recognize the range of artists who transcended it – Anthony Hernandez, but also Bruce Nauman; William Eggleston, but also Louise Lawler –

puts him in a class by himself. Certainly he has understood the import of much of the best art in general, and it shows in his writing and his work. That is why Lewis Baltz, who may or may not be too old to rock today, can enjoy revisiting his closing lines from this nearly thirty-year-old essay:

"*Perhaps…in another thirty years the love affair between America and her photography will blossom once more. Photography will be brought from the shelf and, once again, made much over. And those of us who live long enough can have the 1970s all over again.*"

Happy Birthday Lewis.

Matthew S. Witkovsky
Chair and Ellen and Richard Sandor Curator of Photography
The Art Institute of Chicago

[1] Carl Andre, "Brancusi," M.A. thesis; *Dialogues between Carl Andre and Hollis Frampton* (1962-63), Halifax: Nova Scotia Press, 1972.

Notes on Recent Industrial Developments in Southern California

Typical locations: Previously unimproved land. Proximity to freeways and airports is of primary importance. Secondary consideration is given to the availability of rail and marine transport.

Typical considerations in site selections: Flat land requiring a minimum of grading and which poses no unusual problems in soil or foundation engineering. Typical choices are valley bottoms or the flood plains of rivers. As this type of land is originally often agricultural, the development of one or more large industrial areas may cause severe dislocations in the local economy, such as have occurred in parts of Orange and Santa Clara counties, where agriculture has been almost completely supplanted by the development of industry.

Typical site planning: One developer plans the entire industrial area, usually in conformity with a county or regional master plan. The site is divided into a simple grid of streets and blocks. The grid pattern is broken only at the perimeter of the development, where an encircling frontage road may channel traffic to freeway access or to previously existing surface streets. Broad interior streets are designed to accommodate large numbers of heavy vehicles. Lot sizes, setbacks, and other zoning determinations are incorporated into the master plan and maintained uniformly throughout the development.

Typical construction techniques: A 6" thick concrete slab is poured to form the floor. Concrete slab walls are then poured in forms on the floor slab. These wall slabs are poured in modules. A typical module for a light industrial building would be 18' x 18' with a thickness of 6". Cranes lift these into an upright position along the perimeter of the floor slab, leaving a space of approximately 18" between the edges of the wall modules. Concrete columns are then poured to join the wall modules. These columns often protrude from the exterior surface of the wall and are commonly painted a color different from that of the wall modules as an element of decoration. Roof structure is usually constructed of glue-laminated wood beams. In cases where the area to be spanned is unusually large and the tenant requires that the interior space be free of supporting columns, pre-fabricated roof trusses are employed. Pre-fabricated windows and doors are available in a number of standard sizes. A building of this type, suitable for warehousing or light manufacture, can cost between $11.00 and $50.00 per square foot, depending on the division of the interior spaces and the quality of finish required.

Typical functions: Such developments typically house industries that have become significant in the years since the Korean War. These include: aerospace; data processing and information storage; leisure time industries, such as the fabrication of recreation vehicles and equipment. Often these developments house storage and distribution centers for firms whose manufacturing occurs in other parts of the country or abroad.

Typical names: Often companies tend to select names that obscure the nature of their activities and the identity of their owners. These names are often drawn from the terminology of space exploration, cybernetics, plastics, electronics, and similar new technologies.

Typical environmental relations: Industries that tenant the new industrial parks are often induced to locate there by neighboring communities which regard light industry as an economic asset. Characteristics of heavy manufacturing and extraction industries, such as air, water and noise pollution, unsightly structures, and the necessity of a large unskilled labor force are explicitly absent from the new industries. In contrast, new industries tend to have substantially lower pollution levels; are housed in inoffensive, anonymous structures, often with extensive landscaping; and are staffed by a small, technologically trained labor force, earning middle to upper-middle range salaries.

Typical economic considerations: As these industries provide goods and services of a more highly specialized nature than the older heavy industries, they are therefore more subject to economic fluctuations. Furthermore, as these industries often depend in sum or part upon government contracts, they are vulnerable to changes of priorities in the federal budget even in periods of general economic stability.

This text originally appeared in *Image* (the journal of the George Eastman House) Vol. 17, No.2 (June, 1974): 1-11. Editor's note: This text was published alongside a portfolio of eight images, in addition to one on the cover of *Image*, from Baltz's series *The new Industrial Parks near Irvine, California.* A short text by Eastman House curator William Jenkins accompanied the text, and this publication predates Jenkin's "New Topographics" exhibition (opening in January, 1975) and the release of Baltz's book *The new Industrial Parks near Irvine, California* (in June, 1975).

Landscape Problems

Books about Edward Weston's life and work have become an identifiable sub-category of the photographic publishing industry. Each season summons up new volumes treating one or another aspect of Weston's long and remarkable career; we might expect this trend to accelerate, at least through the centennial of Weston's birth in 1986. Yet despite Weston's undeniable historical importance, Weston has remained a singularly and curiously unfashionable figure among photographers who came to maturity in the last two decades. Some of the reasons for this are obvious. Weston was photography's consummate modernist, an achievement held at discount in a period whose best energies are directed toward deconstructing modernism. Worse yet, to those of us whose sensibilities were formed in the post-war period, Weston's romantic bohemianism seems too studied by half; his life seems to have been lived (and dutifully recorded in his *Daybooks*) in anticipation of the appropriate biographer. Weston's often strident insistence that photography, or a strain of photography, be regarded as high modernist art, sounds pompous now that that struggle has been long won; his passion and individualism seem out of step with today's more detached and collectivist view of the artist's role in society.

Yet for all of this, which is largely true so far as it goes, it's impossible to deny the range and complexity of Weston's achievements as a photographer, or his position in American art in the first half of the twentieth century. And, if it is the romantic and formalist side of Weston's life and work that have captured the admiration of the less critical among his audience, there is substantial evidence in Weston's later work that he was far more than that. The landscape photographs he made beginning around 1935 suggest that Weston had subtly come to reject a purely formalist approach to the landscape. In these later works, most especially those made on his Guggenheim Fellowship and those made for the Limited Editions Book Club's *Leaves of Grass*,[1] Weston demonstrated that he had absorbed many of the same lessons learned by the early expeditionary photographers, forged links with certain works of Atget and Walker Evans, and anticipated many of the concerns that would dominate topographic landscape photography in the 1970's. John Szarkowski noted Weston's development as a landscape photographer in a comparison with Paul Strand: "But before that decade [the 1920's] was out, both Weston, in California, and Paul Strand, on the other edge of the continent, had started again on the problem, beginning with landscape's small parts – a cypress root, a mushroom hidden on the forest floor – and proceeding in measured steps toward the larger chaotic landscape as they learned to recognize and describe progressively complex orders of order.

Of the two, Weston followed the problem farther. Gradually he moved his camera backward to deal with a larger and more complex field. Until the mid-1930's he tended to avoid the horizon, or use it as a beautiful line, a graphic obbligato at the top of the picture, contenting himself with an order that could be managed in a taut, shallow space, almost in two dimensions. But by the late 1930's, when he was at the height of his powers, no space seemed too broad or too deep for him, and he made pictures of the large, complex world that are as clean and clear, as swaggeringly sure of themselves, as his early pictures of the landscape's fragments...He even made landscapes with modern highways in them."[2]

In his latest book Jonathan Green is often more explicit: characterizing Weston's work as "crisp, clean, clear, and literal...It would be difficult to find another photographer of the first half of this century who has eliminated so completely a mystical, symbolical and metaphorical claptrap. The only one who comes close is Walker Evans."

Green concludes: "It has been a common critical belief lately that Evans has been the primary influence of the new color and the New Topographics photographers. This may be true in terms of iconography, but the overriding descriptive influence comes from Weston. For, what we finally feel in his tactile, volumetric, absolutely accurate photographs is a sense of the beauty of the literal fact and a renewed sense of the vigor and possibility of the American dream."[3]

[1] Editor's note: Edward Weston received a Guggenheim Foundation grant in 1937 and 1938. The commission for *Leaves of Grass* was received in 1940, resulting in photographs published in Walt Whitman, *Leaves of Grass*, introduction by Mark Van Doren (New York: The Limited Editions Club, 1942).
[2] John Szarkowski, *American Landscapes* (New York: Museum of Modern Art, 1981).
[3] Jonathan Green, *American Photography: A Critical History Since 1945 to the Present* (New York: H.N. Abrams, 1984).

This text originally appeared in *Aperture*, No. 98 (Spring, 1985).

The Most American Photographer

When Walker Evans died in 1975, his obituary appeared on the first page of *The New York Times.*[1] It was a distinction rarely accorded to any visual artist and even more rarely to a photographer. If a photographer's name became a household word in the United States it was invariably because some aspect of his or her work coincided with the interests of a broader public: Edward Steichen with *The Family of Man*; Ansel Adams with the environmental movement; Richard Avedon with the fantasies of glamour and wealth; Robert Mapplethorpe with Gay Liberation and the AIDS-y Eighties. But Walker Evans was just a photographer, although one might paraphrase Duchamp's judgment on Monet to add, "but *what* a photographer."

For a brief period in the mid-1970s the art market, and the American public in general decided to take photography seriously, and there was no more serious American photographer than Walker Evans. Both his work and his career were exemplary. From the 1920s on Evans made a lifelong project of inventorying the visage of America; his images of cities and towns, buildings and signage, automobiles, faces, styles approached the typological in its thoroughness and anonymity.

Evans' best known work was made in the 1930s for the Farm Security Administration, and published in 1938, under the title *American Photographs*, with a text by Lincoln Kirstein. Later Evans worked as an editor at *Fortune* magazine – where he often assigned himself the most interesting projects – and finished his working life as a Professor at Yale University.

He was the photographer's photographer. His work inspired

adjectives such as detached, ironic, glacial, and rigorous, and the terms were not misapplied. Long before his work was known to the general public it exerted a powerful influence over other American photographers, though in subtle and often hidden ways, which given Evans' character, is probably as he would have wished.

Evans' position was not always so elevated or so assured. Although *American Photographs* remained more or less available since its first printing in 1938, until 1970 the prevailing view of the few critics who paid attention to such things was that Evans was only a more gifted specimen of the American Scene artist that dominated the depression-era and worse, that his gifts had been in decline ever since.

Evans' rehabilitation during the last twenty years was, to a large extent, the work of John Szarkowski, whose 1971 MoMA exhibition and book propelled Evans from the periphery of photographic history toward its center. Other than Evans' own anthologies, the Szarkowski book was, until recently, the definitive statement on Evans' work. Though only one hundred pictures from his encyclopedic œuvre were reproduced in it, their selection and sequencing was inspired, a tribute to and nearly the equal of Evans' justifiably celebrated sequencing of *American Photographs.* Szarkowski's unwavering support was instrumental both in bringing Evans' work to the forefront of the photographic discourse and, even more important, in defining the terms by which it, and all related photographic production would be debated. It could be of interest to consider how and why this came about.

When John Szarkowski assumed the directorship of the Museum of Modern Art's then hegemonic Department of Photography he appeared to have had two ambitious unstated goals. The first was to distinguish his reign from that of his illustrious predecessor, Edward Steichen, while retaining the loyalty of Steichen's constituents; the second was to reinvent the history of twentieth century photography. The rehabilitation of Walker Evans was a central component of this scheme.

Like Evans, Szarkowski was a transplanted Midwesterner and a confirmed Americanist; his esthetic was informed by John Kouwenhoven's celebration of the American vernacular,[2] a world view that favorably compared the Brooklyn Bridge with the cathedrals of Europe and regarded American folk art on a plane with illuminated manuscripts. As a practicing photographer Szarkowski's best-known work had been a study of Louis Sullivan's small-town Midwestern banks, stylistically an homage to Evans. In Szarkowski's point of view Evans was the quintessential nativist photographer, and the leading figure in his campaign to wean American photographic history from its European antecedents and place it in the context of the American *genius loci.* After less than a decade in the bully pulpit of MoMA this part of Szarkowski's project could be judged a success. By the mid-1970s Evans' prestige was enormous – it seemed that almost no ambitious photographic enterprise could be undertaken in America without invoking his name.

Nearly every photographer whose work was exhibited at MoMA, or who received a Guggenheim Fellowship, or was published in a serious journal was one whose work acknowledged Evans' influence and advanced his ideas. This species of photography, which often resembled snapshots in its seeming immediacy unexpected framing, and openness to "bad technique" (blasted highlights, blurred motion, centered subjects, intrusions of the photographer's shadow or reflection, skewed horizons, etc.) was embraced by three generations of photographers; Robert Frank, Garry Winogrand, Lee Friedlander, Tod Papageorge, Henry Wessel and William Eggleston, for example, all built on Evans' legacy. Others drew different inspirations from Evans: Stephen Shore's precise, empty color images of the man-altered landscape; John Gossage's concern with Evans' narrative method; or William Christenberry's labored retracing of Evans' footsteps throughout the South. *New Topographics* was in some part indebted to Evans as was, if one agrees with Jean-François Chevrier, the one-time conceptual artist Dan Graham. Through William Eggleston Evans' influence reached the U.K. and can be felt in the entire enterprise of what has been called The New British Color, most notably in the work of its most thoughtful practitioner, Paul Graham, whose immensely subtle works echo some of Evans' meticulous attention to significant detail. Traces of Evans' infused Arthur Penn's *Bonnie and Clyde* and nearly overwhelm Jim Jarmusch's *Down by Law.* When appropriation artist Sherrie Levine selected Evans' classic images for her conceptual pieces – titled *After Walker Evans* – one might say that his work had come full circle.

Levine gives us a clue to Evans' stature – she could, after all, have appropriated from anyone she wished. Evans' images are now icons, and the great photographer of monuments has himself become a monument. The only real question pending now is what, if anything, in this well-digested artist's practice is relevant to the present situation.

1994 is not an especially propitious year to evaluate Evans' reputation. The current political climate, at least in the United States, militates against the valorization of any white male liberal.

Worse, Evans' tribe has not increased: since 1977 no new names have been added to the honor roll of his followers. And, yet worse, the entire enterprise of photography as understood and practiced by Evans and his followers is in terminal crisis. Nothing has come recently to replenish Evans' tradition and it doesn't seem likely that anything will. The action moved elsewhere.

One of the more important elsewheres was critical theory, which might be considered to be the art of our time. For the moment Evans may be doomed to the fate of being just another poor clueless wretch who had the supreme ill fortune to have lived and worked before post-Structuralist theory had delivered the necessary tools for serious critical inquiry. Critical theory takes no prisoners: Evans has already become academic cannon fodder.

Yet certain features of Evans' practice, as well as many of his reflections on it, seem to show that he was keenly self-aware and not at all oblivious to the judgment of the future. A gifted dissembler, Evans pursued his own agenda; taking the FSA's dollar (cheating a bit along the way) he never confused his goals with theirs.

The stated agenda of the FSA was propaganda: to publicize the plight of the rural poor in order to mobilize public opinion in support of New Deal relief and recovery programs. Evans had no special quarrel with this, but he was after something else. He intended to leave a more profound and more enduring artistic legacy than the centrist reform politics of the Roosevelt administration. Evans' mentors were neither Marx, nor Jane Hull, nor Lewis Hine; they were more likely Balzac and Stendahl. Photography, for Evans, was neither document nor art, but a kind of novel; a means to create a literature of images, using facts to construct fictions that revealed truths. It was a huge ambition, and his use of photography, or photographic images, was similar to the use of images in narrative cinema. So far as "art photography" was concerned, Evans was openly scornful. Though falling short of Joseph Kosuth's dictum that it makes little or no difference what a work of art looks like, Evans' disdain for the conventions of the 'fine photograph' was in sharp opposition to his "arty" contemporaries.

At the heart of Evans' ideology was his belief in a natural nobility, the Jeffersonian ideal of The New Democratic Man, nurtured in liberty and equal to the great tasks of his age. It was a notion that had had its ups and downs in American history but in the wake of the Great Depression gained a new relevance. It implied that in a democracy there existed the potential for ordinary people to overcome injustice and to redeem a world ravaged by economic collapse. At odds with Marxism, this view did not valorize a specific class – though it tilted toward the dispossessed. Such an ideology seems fuzzy compared with "scientific socialism" and, yet like it, hopelessly utopian. That the world would unfold differently was not for Evans to know.

Conventional wisdom has cast Evans as the Great Documentarian; and Szarkowski reframed this in modernist terms. In fact, the evidence for both views are as arguable as are the terms themselves. If Evans was a documentarian it was only to the degree that all representations are, in some sense, documents, to the degree that they reflect the world in which they were made. Robert Mapplethorpe's demi-monde fantasies, Garry Winogrand's cinéma-véritée and Martha Rosler's image/text can all be said to hold equal claims to being documentary, which is, in effect, to empty the category of any useful meaning. And if Evans were a modernist he was certainly not a vulgar modernist, that is, with a market-driven claim to the stylistically defined transcendent object. Evans might be considered a modernist in another sense: that his work is, by its nature, a meditation of the conditions of its own existence, and the relativism of that condition, although that position is currently claimed as post-modernist.

Evans' own attitude toward the document was clearly stated and well known: he claims to have chosen to work in *the documentary style*, which indicates that he was aware of the relativism of style itself. "Documentary" was only one choice on a long menu of equally viable representational constructs, but it was the one which best suited his project. Afterwards, photographers concerned with grounding their work in authenticity would make more extravagant claims for the document, *per se*, and invoke Evans in their support, but this is a willful misreading of his stated intentions.

The main problem which critics and viewers of Evans' work have to confront is moral rather than esthetic: namely Evans and The Question of the Other. Aloof and uninvited, Evans imposed himself and his vision on his subjects, he appropriated their images for purposes unknown to them and he made them speak with his voice. We presently regard such behavior as politically incorrect.

The 1930s had a different though equally rigorous idea of political correctness, which presupposed the political immaturity of the masses and the obligation of the intelligentsia to lead them in their struggle for empowerment. That a few individuals were traduced in the process was regrettable but inevitable in the pursuit of a greater social vision. This assumption was shared by the Fascists, the Comintern, and the New Deal, and remains tacitly in favor today.

Progressive documentary photographic practice has reversed itself since Evans' time. We comprehend and represent the world in a radically different way than we did before Walter Benjamin, focusing our attention as much, or more, on representational codes as on the nominal subject. While Evans, I believe, had a rather sophisticated understanding of the opacity and relativity of his medium, it was not his chief area of interrogation.

Evans' works speak from and for not only another time but, for many of his appreciators, another place. Like Melville, Whitman, Emerson and Hopper, Evans portrayed something uniquely American in a distinctly American idiom, describing an experience shared only vicariously by Europeans.

Interest in Evans arrived late to Europe, late enough, ironically to coincide with a somewhat diminished attention in the United States. (Of the twenty-six monographs by or about Evans published between 1930 and 1989, only two were of European origin; of the eleven published since, six were European, one American with a European author and four American.) Reflecting this recent European interest are two publications, both organized by French authors, each shedding different lights on Evans' intentions.

The first, *Walker Evans and Dan Graham*, is the catalogue of an exhibition of the same name originated in 1992 at the Witte de With Museum in Rotterdam and circulating to a number of venues, among them the Whitney Museum of American Art.[3] The point of this exhibition and book is to demonstrate the hitherto unsuspected relationship between the two artists, a formidable task insofar as one suspects that this rapport was unguessed by the artists themselves. While it is likely that Evans and Graham might have been aware of each other's work, it seems even more likely that the great classic photographer and the well-known conceptual artist had no special interest in each other. With the exception of an excellent essay by Alan Sekula, "Walker Evans and the Police," the book tilts heavily toward an explication of Graham's largely unpublished photographic works from the 1960s and 70s. Benjamin H. D. Buchloh's text on Graham's progress is correct, while the introductory text, by Jean-François Chevrier is, to use a word usually connected to Hollywood musical comedies, zany.

A more recent, and more lavish Evans project is Gilles Mora's comprehensive study whose English title is (unfortunately, I believe) *Walker Evans: The Hungry Eye.*[4] Though lacking both Chevrier's swashbuckling academic swordsmanship or Szarkowski's special affinity for Evans' work, Mora's book is more than just workmanlike. With over 350 images it is not the most exhaustive compilation of Evans' work, (two earlier American publications hold that distinction), but Mora's passion for Evans, though controlled, is evident, as he details, period by period and subject by subject, Evans' nearly fifty year working life. Mora is no revisionist; he accepts and extends the received view of Evans, but does so with an attention to the nuances of Evans' project that supports the book's implicit claim to be indispensable for Evans scholars. Perhaps a bit short on theory, the book is long on facts: it seems that Mora misses nothing. Lacking any special covert agenda, *The Hungry Eye* is pure Evans and is as interesting, or not, as one finds his work. It seems that it was Mora's ambition to make the definitive book on Evans, and for the moment he has probably succeeded.

It will probably be several years before another Evans hagiography is required. In both Europe and America, the future of Evans scholarship will, to the extent it exists at all, be more in the line of the Chevrier book, though hopefully more plausible, that is, a re-evaluation of Evans' practice to discover, or create, a lineage for a contemporary artist or movement. What may be interesting, perhaps astonishing, will be to see if Evans will be as infinitely recyclable in the future as he has been in the past, and, if so, to what ends his work will be used.

[1] Editor's note: Walker Evans' obituary, written by Alden Whitman, ran in the April 11, 1975 edition of *The New York Times.*

[2] Editor's note: See John A. Kouwenhoven, *Made in America: The Arts in Modern Civilization* (New York: Doubleday, 1948).

[3] Jean-Francois Chevrier, *Walker Evans & Dan Graham* (Rotterdam: Witte de With; New York: Whitney Museum of American Art, 1992).

[4] Gilles Mora, *Walker Evans: The Hungry Eye* (New York: H.N. Abrams, 1993).

This text originally appeared in *The Times Literary Supplement,* London, 4 March 1994, 10-11.

The New West

There is something paradoxical in the way that documentary photographs interact with our notions of reality. To function at all as documents they must first persuade us that they describe their subject accurately and objectively. In fact their initial task is to convince their audience that they truly are documents, and that the photographer has exercised his powers of observation and description rather than his imaginings and prejudices. The ideal photographic document would appear to be without author or art. But photographs, despite their verisimilitude, are abstractions; their information is selective and incomplete. The power of the documentary photograph resides in its ability to inform as well as reflect our perceptions of the external world. Because of this it becomes possible, for example, to marvel at the striking resemblance the rural South still bears to Walker Evans photographs from the 1930's.

Few photographers have demonstrated as sophisticated an understanding of this as Robert Adams, whose recent book, *The New West*, is a model of excellence in documentary photography. His subject is the suburban strip development that has proliferated along the eastern face of the Rocky Mountains from Wyoming to New Mexico during the past twenty years. Adams has infused his vision of Colorado – the relation of its inhabited parts to its mountains and prairies – with the authority of absolute fact, yet his style of picture making also offers a complex moral understanding of his subject.

Adams claims pioneer photographer Timothy O'Sullivan as an antecedent; one might add William Henry Jackson who, like

O'Sullivan, also worked in the same terrain a century before Adams. More recent photographic practice offers few parallels to Adams' work, the closest being the use of photographic documentation in the work of certain conceptual artists, such as Ed Ruscha's books, or the industrial typologies of Bernd and Hilla Becher, all of whom have a shared interest in the efficiency of photographic information.

What distinguishes Adams from most of his photographic contemporaries is the distance he takes from his subject, both literally and figuratively. This distance is essential to Adams project which is to present a record of man's attempts to live on, and occasionally with, the land, a theme reduced to kitschy sentimentality by his immediate predecessors. His subject requires honesty as well as distance, and his work abounds in both. It is this forthright and (seemingly) disengaged quality of Adams' vision that permits him to direct our attention to the most squalid and meretricious instances of commercial development without reveling in their Pop vulgarity. More, Adams' rigor and detachment sets the stage for his hard-edged humanism; Adams may be a moralist, but in *The New West* he refuses to scold or preach.

The suburban vistas that opened in America after World War II and with the GI Bill overwhelmed traditional urbanism with the speed and the extent of their growth. Conceived in expedience for the sole purpose of turning a quick buck, hopelessly dependent on the automobile, new non-cities have disposed themselves formlessly along the frontage roads of most of our Interstate Highways. Posing an ecological threat that is only now being taken into account, the sprawl-city is as hostile to genuine urbanism as it is to the land it recklessly consumes. For as much as the landscape is deformed by the encroaching suburban juggernaut, traditional urban (*i.e. civilized*) values are equally under attack; American civil culture, never so very deep, disappears if spread too thin.

Adams shows us how ephemeral these man made structures seem to be and how uneasily they rest on Colorado's high plains: trailer parks and tract houses that promise no bulwark against the arid and inhospitable land they occupy so uneasily. It is impossible to associate the idea of 'home' or 'shelter' with these constructions; rather, they most resemble the test structures built near the Ground Zero nuclear testing site.

The sheer pervasiveness of suburban development has engaged architects, planners, urban theorists, conservationists, sociologists, novelists and social critics of all persuasions, and lately, photographers. Each has emphasized a different aspect of suburbia's virtues or shortcomings and the recent books on the subject could fill a good-sized shelf, with Venturi and Scott Brown's celebration of Las Vegas on one end and Bill Owens' ugly and patronizing *Suburbia* on the other.[2] *The New West* is a unique and valuable contribution to this collection; thus far no other book has so compellingly demonstrated the mutuality of intrusion between the landscape and its inhabitants, or so clearly shown why we should be paying attention. "Why open our eyes anywhere but in undamaged places like national parks?... We also need to see the whole geography, natural and man-made..."[3]

For Adams the redeeming quality of the western landscape is its light, falling equally on mountaintop and used car lot, a tarnished metaphor of divine grace. But a less redemptive reading is also possible: a light that is hard and glaring, with little shade or comfort, a perpetual noon that magnifies each flaw of a desiccated and tired land.

Claude Levi-Strauss observed that America's cities suffered from "a chronic illness...a high temperature...which prevents them, for all of their everlasting youthfulness, from ever being entirely well."[4] Without quite knowing it, Americans seem to be aware of this, and arrange their cities and their lives to provide themselves with maximum insulation from communal space and from each other. Adams shows us this side of the city only too well, as a collection of artifacts rather than of personalities. His chosen subjects are the reflective windows, the freeway verges, and the empty lots that define our common urban heritage. Adams' stylistic signature is to isolate his subjects in the center of a passive, square frame resulting in an extremely static image, appropriate for the representation of a topography in which little is animate.

People are conspicuous by their absence in *The New West*, and its few inhabitants stand as representatives of a larger category of equally anonymous individuals. When they are depicted they are engaged in activities so banal as to foreclose any possibility of individuality: the tasks they perform – shopping, driving a car, hanging out the wash – are so routinized as to suggest that Adams could have made an identical photograph on any day he chose. These kind of images seems to be the counterinstance of the 'decisive moment', with Adams willingly trading one of photography's most dramatic attributes, that of isolating a specific action out of the flux of time, for something less inherently theatrical but equally potent: the rigor of scientific observation.

Adams' insistence on the ordinary and typical, as well as the suggestion that his work is experientially verifiable, acts as a prophylactic strategy against our culture's increasing suspicion that photographs, if not outright lies, are at best naïve distortions of reality. Confining his attentions to the most ubiquitous subjects and events, and photographing in a modest and reticent manner, Adams constructs a series of correspondences between the viewer's experience of the world and the world that Adams proposes in his pictures. This offer of mutual trust lays the foundation for Adams to assert a point in which he strongly believes, and one that falls outside the boundaries of rational discourse: that in spite of all evidence to the contrary, there is a pure and glacial beauty that still resides in our wounded landscape.

[1] Robert Venturi, Denise Scott Brown and Steven Izenouri, *Learning from Las Vegas* (Cambridge: The MIT Press, 1972). Bill Owens, *Suburbia* (San Francisco: Straight Arrow Books, 1973)

[2] Editor's note: The quote comes from Robert Adams' opening inscription in *The New West*, op. cit.

[3] Claude Levi-Strauss, *Tristes Tropiques*, trans. John Russell (New York: Criterion Books, 1961) 101.

This text originally appeared in *Art In America,* Vol. 63, No. 2 (March-April, 1975): 41-43. The essay is a review of Robert Adams' *The New West* (Boulder: Colorado Associated University Press, 1974).

Notes on *Park City*

Park City is a rapidly growing resort, suburb and second home development 27 miles east of Salt Lake City in Utah's Wasatch Mountains. State Highway 224 connects Park City with Interstate 80, which passes within six miles of the town's northern boundary.

Downtown Salt Lake City is a 35-minute drive in good weather. The original mining settlement lies in a north-south canyon less than two miles long and one-half mile wide and was founded in the late 1860's when deposits of silver were discovered nearby. The mining boom lasted until 1898 when a fire destroyed most of the town. Although Park City was rebuilt, the fire marked the end of an era. Diminishing returns from the mines resulted in a downturn in the local economy that lasted into the 1950's. Park City was in the process of becoming a ghost town.

The burgeoning interest in skiing brought the beginnings of an economic recovery. Ski runs and lifts were developed on the mountains north and west of Park City and hotels and restaurants were opened in the old town. Good skiing conditions, a picturesque Old West setting, and thousands of undeveloped acres close to town suggested to investors that Park City could be developed along the same lines as Aspen, Colorado.

By 1977 Park City's second boom was underway, with large-scale residential developments planned or in construction immediately north of the Old Town. Six increments of detached housing were in various stages of completion, as well as several condominiums, a shopping center, a resort hotel, convention facilities and two golf courses. Prior to construction most of his land had been open range, although one tract near town had been a dump for mining wastes. It was in this area that some of the most ambitious development was taking place, and it was there that I most worked extensively in 1978 and 1979.

The choice of Park City as a subject was my attempt to describe the creation of a typical new western town, rather than single out Park City for invidious distinction. After all, most of us born in the west after WWII live in structures similar to those being built in Park City. It is only because Park City is typical that it exerts a claim on our attention – that and the convenient fact that so much diverse, intensive development was visible at several stages in a contained location. Nevertheless, cities that rise out of the western desert overnight always seem to carry with them the eerie possibility that they might vanish as quickly as they appeared.

When I first saw Park City it was the land, rather than the structures, that held my interest. Other than in films and photographs of natural catastrophes – or in disaster movies – I had never seen a landscape so bleak, blasted and chaotic. Much of the land was churned and pocked, littered with fragments of wood, twisted wire, rusted metal and broken glass, and supported only the sparsest vegetation. The appearance of "matter out of place" was only partly attributable to the detritus of mining and, later, construction; even the land that had thus far escaped both waves of development looked preternaturally silent and dead. The overall impression was one of purposeless, violent, destruction. During the two and one half years that I worked in Park City that impression never wholly left me and much that I saw later reinforced it.

Joan Didion, in a review of Norman Mailer's *Executioner's*

Song (which is partly set in Utah) wrote: "the very subject [of Mailer's book] is that vast emptiness at the center of the Western experience, a nihilism antithetical not only to literature but to most other forms of human endeavor, a dread so close to zero that human voices fade out, trail off, like skywriting. Beneath what Mailer calls "the immense blue of the strong sky of the American West... not too much makes a difference."[1]

Beneath the world of boom-time optimism, the condition of the land suggested a sense of ultimate futility. It was no mystery why the land looked as it did. Many of the construction sites were on land previously used as a dump for mining wastes. The age of these dump sites did little to mitigate the appearance of destruction; with time, wind and water further pulverized the soil. The land held a visible record of its use, and the residue had its own order that was neither pictorial, nor non-pictorial. As a photographic subject it was self-structured and any attempt to impose another layer of order would be gratuitous.

If this sounds as though I'm suggesting that I decided to simply level the camera and point at the horizon, that is substantially correct, certainly so far as the first 19 elements of *Park City* are concerned. The formal qualities of these images echo an order implicit in the scene in front of the camera, an esthetic similar to the NASA photographs of the surface of Mars.

If photographs automatically formalize their content, as is claimed, then the formal qualities of the photograph can be taken for granted as a condition of the photographs being, and the discussion of formalism as an intentional esthetic posture would be academic. What may not be academic is the way in which photographic form reflects and describes the forms and events of the phenomenal world.

Photographs apprehend the surfaces of the world fixed in viewpoint and time, specific surfaces whose literalness and immediacy make it difficult to extrapolate accurate and reasonable generalizations about the world that exists outside its borders. Which is a way of saying that individual photographs often give a very limited and tendentious view of external reality. Better, I reasoned, a series of images that could, in a sense, surround its subject and give some better sense of it. In *Park City*, as in most of my previous works, the series, and not the individual image is the unit of work. Working in series allows points to be raised, asserted through repetition, critiqued, restructured into subcategories; a visual syntax can be evolved to show a number of facets of the same subject. The effect is comparable with non-narrative film, a "paper movie," to use Larry Sultan's phrase. And, while one "frame" might be more interesting, or esthetically appealing, than another, each is of equal importance and each relies on the context of the total work to achieve significance. The individual image, removed from its context in the group, is a fragment.

Ideally in such a project, the photographer should be invisible and the medium transparent, and I aspire to that level of objectivity. I intend that this work be neutral and uninflected and as free as I can make them from esthetic or ideological posturing. The photographs in *Park City* are made to conform to the conventions of ordinary seeing. I do this in the hope that the works will be seen as factual statements about their subject rather than expressions of the artist's attitudes.

Each image is titled with its exact location, an implicit invitation to a viewer to visit the scene and judge its veracity for him or herself.[2] Equally, the viewer is invited to consider the context from which the image was taken, as much significant information is about what takes place outside the borders of the image. My technique is based on the idea of showing the subject with the maximum possible precision and clarity. In many of the *Park City* images important information exists in small details, or is seen at a distance, which is the reason for my choice of a high-definition image. I attempted to give equal emphasis to each area of the image, privileging no one area at the expense of another, to permit the viewer to select from an array of democratically rendered information, rather than have the emphasis pre-selected.[3]

Above all, I wanted my work to convey the uncanny clarity of the high altitude light that bathes Park City. Crisp and hard-edged outlines go unsoftened by atmospheric perspective. The fact is of being in a vacuum; each object seems to be fixed in its own discrete space as though the space in the photographs was discontinuous. The interiors shared this quality of airlessness, though in their case the effect was confining and claustrophobic. Recently I showed my work from Park City to Walter Hopps whose opinions I value. After looking at the work rather thoroughly he remarked that landscape was a particularly modern concern in Western art. The remark struck me because, on an instant's reflection, it was so evidently true that I felt embarrassed not to have thought of it before.

What I understood him to mean was in the approximately 20,000 years that people have been making images of their gods, their animals, and each other, it has been only in the last four centuries that landscape, other than as a backdrop for figures, has appeared in art. Only after certain historical developments took place could the land be thought of as a suitable object for esthetic contemplation. Among these developments, the most prominent was the evolution away from the land as the primary site of economic production. As the agrarian model was eroded by its industrial successor, it became possible to take the distance necessary to contemplate the land as 'landscape'. (This change took place in a broader climate of the decline of a religio-mystical worldview, the ascendance of Empiricism and, following from that, reawakened interest in the secular and material world).

The reason to raise this question at all is to point out that our response to nature, which it pleases most of us as to regard as somehow intrinsic ('natural') is in reality a cultural artifact of the industrial revolution.

Our understanding of the landscape is a consequence of industrialism in two important ways. The first, and most obvious, is that in most of the world, and in the entire developed world, industrial technologies have physically altered the landscape. One need only think of the Los Angeles basin to see this, although it's hard to imagine that there is a place in the US, or Western Europe, or Japan that one could not find some evidence of industrialism or its waste products.

But more subtle and more pervasive is the fact that our responses to landscape are conditioned by our experience as inhabitants of an industrial society, insofar as since that society inculcates in us the values that we project upon nature.

In Plato's *Phaedrus*, Phaedrus asks Socrates why he never ventures beyond the gates of the city, and Socrates replies that he looks for wisdom among men and not in the trees or the countryside. The implication is clear: that nature is barren of meaning or ideas, and so it was for Socrates who sought ethical wisdom. Were a contemporary of ours to dismiss nature as a source of knowledge we would find him either ignorant or perverse. In our culture, which holds ethical wisdom at a discount, the systematic observation of natural phenomena is the cornerstone of our science, and science is the supreme achievement of our culture. Interest in the natural world is good business and in a capitalist society that argument is usually sufficient.

Yet it is far from incorrect to think of the natural 'wilderness' as moral wilderness as well. Nature is morally neutral and seems to accommodate almost any system of beliefs imposed upon it (at least until recently).

One of the most common views capitalist society takes of nature is among the most rigorous and most appalling, "Landscape as Real-Estate."[4] This was the view of nature presented to me in Park City and the viewpoint I showed in my photographs.

To know that an apparently unbroken expanse of land is overlaid with invisible lines demarcating ownership and indicating the pattern of future development is to perceive it in a very different way than one would otherwise. That these divisions only coincidentally pertain to topography and are the arbitrary result of financial speculation, illustrates the casually rapacious disdain that our culture has of the natural world as such.

This attitude holds all non-productive land as marginal; 'nature' is what's left over after every other demand has been satisfied. That the land offers our society such an excellent arena for its venality tells us much about what is distinctly 'modern' in landscape. Nonetheless it would be simplistic to suggest that our culture's view of nature is no more complex than sheer greed. Nature elicits other responses from us, responses that expose the contradictions between our actions and our image of ourselves.

We see nature both instrumentally and as a refuge from our instrumentality; our systems of production mirror processes found in nature, yet we respond to each quite differently. When we are in awe of nature's processes it is because, rather than in spite of, nature's remoteness from human purpose. Nature is, intrinsically, elsewhere; nature has nothing to do with us; her back is turned way. To contemplate the ordinary landscape is a form of gazing into the abyss, absent any implication of fascination or horror. Nature's opacity seems a possible refuge from our own subjectivity, yet, somehow, we never really seem to close with nature. We might choose to believe, as did Rilke, that through the medium of art the landscape and man find one another. Yet this argument, for all its obvious appeal seems based more in hope than fact. Perhaps it is because we have less confidence in the power of our arts, or perhaps it is that we have come to understand that our estrangement is beyond reconciliation. This, I believe, is what is 'modern' in the landscape.

[1] Joan Didion, "I Want to Go Ahead and Do It," *The New York Times*, Oct. 7, 1979.

[2] As one artist and critic, Mario Pfeiffer, recently did, not with *Park City*, but with *The new Industrial Parks near Irvine, California*. Editor's note: See Pfeiffer, *Reconsidering The new Industrial Parks near Irvine, California by Lewis Baltz, 1974* (Berlin: Sternberg Press, 2011).

[3] Joe Deal, several years later, coined the term 'optical democracy.' I wish I had.

[4] I am indebted to Marvin Heiferman for the phrase "Landscape as real estate."

This text originally appeared in *Landscape: Theory*, ed. Carol Di Grappa (New York: Lustrum Press, 1980) 23-39. Editor's note: The text was written in relation to the photographs that would comprise Lewis Baltz's *Park City* (Albuquerque: Artspace Press, and New York: Castelli Graphics, 1980).

American Photography in the 1970s: Too Old To Rock, Too Young To Die

Some events pass more quickly in America than in Europe. The British Century, from Waterloo to Sarajevo, very nearly spanned its allotted ten decades; the American Century dispensed with itself in only three. Those thirty years were bracketed by two iconic images, the first of US Marines raising the American flag on Mount Suribachi in February 1945, the second of another American flag, folded and wrapped in plastic, being carried by the United States Ambassador to Cambodia, John Gunther Dean, as he walked out of Phnom Penh a few days before Khmer Rouge forces captured the city.[1] The first image was one of the most widely reproduced photographs of its time. The second, portraying an equally historic moment, was not.

The two photographs reflect some of the innumerable ways that America's realities and perceptions changed over those thirty years, as well as the changed status of photography. In 1945 Americans communicated the appearance of the world's great events to each other through the medium of still photography; by 1975, by and large, they did not, and not even the recrudescence of the Lazarus-like *Life* magazine could gainsay that difference.

By the 1970s still photographs, so far as they could be claimed to document anything, recorded a more evanescent subject: America's sense of itself. Yet despite the shift from a mass audience to a more limited one – the word 'elite' does not really apply – the 1970s witnessed an intensity of photographic activity in America unequalled since the 1930s, and an acceptance of photography as a major medium of expression unparalleled in our history. Photography was one of the brighter spots in that otherwise bleak decade. It is not more engaging to think of the 1970s as the years between Diane Arbus and Cindy Sherman than to remember them as the decade that began with the Kent State killings and ended with the election of Ronald Reagan?

In the 1970s a number of institutions came into existence, or came to the height of their powers, that materially affected the enterprise of American photography. The most pervasive of these was the system of higher education. In 1945 very few photographers held academic degrees in photography or the fine arts; in 1975 most of those styling themselves photographers or artists were able to do so on the strengths of such academic credentials.

During the 1970s college and university offerings in the fine arts, and most especially in photography, metastasized at both the graduate and undergraduate levels, finding a place in the most respected institutions in the land. Princeton University endowed a chair in the History of Photography and Modern Art, and Yale University endowed a chair in the practice of photography. Even more crimson dowager of American universities, Harvard, while officially cleaving to the traditional line that the history of art is a proper subject of academic interest while its practice is not, none the less offered courses in the practice of photography taught by both resident faculty and distinguished visitors. Oddly enough, in view of such interests at the highest levels of the Ivy League, the most successful and prestigious program in photography was at the University of New Mexico, which attracted artists and scholars from around the nation and the world, many of whom would go elsewhere and initiate similar programmes in other universities.

Expanding enrollment and expanding employment in the university system (including both private and public colleges and universities, art schools, and two-year colleges) meant that higher education was becoming both major educator and employer of serious photographers. It is probable that teaching had supplanted commercial or magazine work as the 'other' work of most serious photographers by the mid-1970s; especially outside New York where relatively few opportunities existed for the newly-made Master of Fine Arts other than to return as an employee to the system he or she had just left. Such academic recidivism (teachers teaching students to become teachers who would teach students to become teachers *ad infinitum*) was only imaginable in a rapidly expanding sector of a healthy economy. Needless to say it did not last into the 1980s.

While the system was expanding, its benefits were obvious. For the student financial support and, in the 1960s and early 1970s, some shelter from military conscription – the war in Vietnam had made a generation of scholars. For the professor a secure, if not large pay cheque, an employer more tolerant of artistic freedoms than most, and a power base of sorts. The drawback was that most of this produced a photography that was academic in the most unflattering sense of that word.[2]

One of the most salutary effects upon photography of this willy-nilly schooling was, as John Szarkowski noted,[3] not to serve but to create a need. The thousands of students who encountered photography as a fine art, officially encouraged in the highest halls of learning – even those with the good sense to seek their vocations elsewhere – would nevertheless retain something from that contact and might come to form the nucleus of an educated, critical, informed and demanding audience for serious photography. As yet, the goal has been met only imperfectly. Nevertheless it does represent a small step toward the creation of such an audience. And if that audience exists anywhere, European friends would have us believe it is here in America, however far short it has fallen of our best expectations.

Another institution that was seminal in the support of American photography during the 1970s was the National Endowment for the Arts, a Federal agency chartered to provide public funding for the arts in the United States. Originally discussed seriously during the Kennedy administration, it, like so many Kennedy proposals, became a reality only after his death. And, like so many Kennedy programmes passed into law under Lyndon B. Johnson, languished in relative obscurity. After a lacklustre White House Festival of the Arts in 1965, with poet Robert Lowell and photographer Paul Strand publically refusing to attend, LBJ's ardour for the arts was dampened. Guns, butter, *and* culture seemed to strain our resources too far.

Ironically, it was during the Nixon administration that the NEA began to receive the massive funding that made it the major single factor in American cultural life during the 1970s. Ironic, because of Nixon's well-advertised loathing for the intelligentsia, who had returned his contempt since his early days as a Red-baiting junior Congressman. Reliable sources have it that one of Nixon's advisers suggested that he neutralize the American cultural community by the time-honoured method of buying them off – at an annual cost vastly less expensive that a few hours of war-making in Indio-China. For whatever reason, and with whatever hopes, Nixon agreed to fund the NEA at a level that would make it the most visible presence in American cultural life. The intelligentsia accepted the money and continued to despise Nixon.

One corollary to this was that funding for the arts, if it was to reflect credit on the administration, must be free of any partisan political influence; must be, in fact, above any such suspicion. Toward that end the NEA was staffed by outstanding professionals, whose loyalties were demonstratably toward furthering the arts in America than toward the government, and it remained the least politicized of any federal agency. It resembled in parts both the Canadian and British Art Councils, although at its zenith its funding surpassed either.

As a photographer one often felt that there was an unstated attitude, if not policy, of affirmative action toward those mediums least able to survive in the private sector: artists' films, video, performance, and, especially, photography. In its heyday the NEA funded programmes – often several in each category – to sponsor the making, exhibition, publishing, public collecting, and criticism of photographs by living Americans. So pervasive was government funding that one wit suggested an 'audience participation' grant: close the circle of funding random citizens to go and look at all this product. It is good to remember when such an observation could still be humorous: with the triumph of the know-nothing wing of the Republican party and the election of Ronald Reagan to the Presidency in 1980, funding for the arts was sharply reduced. The NEA remains intact today, but with far less influence than it had in the previous decade, and one doubts that even the valiant souls who steer this ship through its present stormy seas would really argue that it is now merely a tighter, 'leaner' vessel.

A major recipient of assistance from the National Endowment for the Arts was American museums, and nowhere was the effect of this funding more evident that in the area of photographic exhibitions and collections. A number of American museums, including some of the most respected, had an historical commitment to photography in the arts, but the avalanche of interest in the 1970s made nearly every American museum desirous of making, if not a full programme, at least a respectable showing in the area of fine-art photography. Photography was relatively inexpensive to exhibit, acquire, and ship. It had a broad public appeal that did not go unnoticed by museum directors eager to report expanding attendances. And, finally, it was becoming fashionable in the most elite art circles. The 1960s had brought a building boom to the museum world, and a number of cities had impressive edifices without correspondingly impressive collections or exhibitions schedules. Photography was part of the solution to that problem.

In the 1950s and 60s a handful of museums dominated the exhibition and collection of photography, most notably the Museum of Modern Art in New York and the George Eastman House in Rochester. Other museums were usually content to accept the often excellent circulating exhibitions that these two leaders organized. NEA funding, more than any other single reason, broke this monopoly. If the NEA had any stated bias it was against the aggregation of culture in one metropolitan centre and in favour of a regional, pluralistic approach to the arts. With NEA assistance regional museums could organize their own exhibitions, become exporters rather than importers of photographic attitudes and works; and most took advantage of this opportunity, using NEA funds as seed money to develop local interest and support in photographic programmes.

Two museum persons dominated the discourse that surrounded the exhibition of contemporary photography in the United States during the 1970s; both were, themselves, photographers. John Szarkowski, at the Museum of Modern Art, New York, and Van Deren Coke, at George Eastman House 1970-3, University Art Museum, University New Mexico, Albuquerque, 1973-9 and at the San Francisco Museum of Modern Art from 1979 onward, were the two leading figures whose views defined the range of mainstream contemporary curatorial attitudes toward photography in the 1970s. Szarkowski favoured photography in the documentary style, with a special interest in the American vernacular; Coke was more internationalist, his interest lying more in the areas of cross-fertilization between photography and the other visual arts. Taking nothing away from the efforts of other distinguished scholars and curators, there were no other museum figures who either by temperament or position exerted such a strong influence on American photography during the 1970s and beyond.

Outside the sphere of established museums, and often even more reliant upon public funding, were alternative spaces, though in America these venues play a far less important role than in the U.K. Conceived as exhibition halls for works too non-commercial for private galleries and too radical, politically or stylistically, for established museums, alternative spaces for photography turned out, for the most part, to be a disappointment, exhibiting work that was identical in kind, if not quality, to that of their more established counterparts. The effect was less to challenge prevailing attitudes than to institutionalize them even in their less accomplished manifestations.

Most of the conditions favouring photography in America in

the 1970s would be familiar, in some degree, to photographic audiences in any modern industrial democracy. But the development of a large, active, private market for contemporary photography would be quite unfamiliar. And no surprise: before the 1970s it was almost unheard of even in America.

In 1969 the late Lee Witkin opened the first commercially viable New York art gallery devoted exclusively to the exhibition and sale of photographs as fine art. To the surprise of most, he prospered. Two years later Light Gallery opened its doors on New York's fashionable upper Madison Avenue, dedicated to an equally daring proposition, the exhibition and sale of the works of living photographers. Light, too, flourished throughout the decade. Similar galleries began appearing in New York, as well as Washington, DC, Los Angeles, Chicago, Boston, Houston, San Francisco, Seattle and other regional centres.

More important in the taking of photography out of its ghetto was its incorporation into the exhibition programme of the most prestigious painting and sculpture galleries during the 1970s: Castelli, 1971; Ileana Sonnabend Gallery, 1972; Pace Editions, 1973; John Weber Gallery, 1974; Marlborough Gallery, 1975; Prakapas Gallery and Robert Miller Gallery in 1977. Other galleries followed. While it was extremely difficult to see photographs exhibited as art on New York galleries walls in 1967, by 1977 it was extremely difficult not to.

With a few stunning and well-publicized exceptions, the economic consequences for most photographers was slight. More important was the new aura of respectability, attendant on any enterprise in America that is perceived to be lucrative. That, and an inchoate hope for the future: if things continued to go as they had, a serious photographer might someday be able to earn, from the sale of his or her artwork, a living commensurate with that of an automobile mechanic or university lecturer. Events gave the lie to this overly sanguine view of the future; it gave heart to women and men who were doing as they always had and always would, supporting their photographic activity with jobs in other, remunerative fields.

The market interest in photography prompted a new level of media interest. Important art journals allocated ever-increasing editorial space to photography. The apotheosis of this was the September 1976 issue of the leading establishment art journal, *Artforum*, which was devoted entirely to photography. The lofty New York Times regularly published critiques of current photography exhibitions, as did the somewhat less lofty Village Voice. Both were, in very different ways, national newspapers, and the effect of this coverage was felt far outside New York City.

But none of this adequately answers two questions: why photography? And why now? No one answer can suffice, but an observation by Marvin Heiferman, then Director of Castelli, sounds as plausible as any. The art world, he said, seems to have a cyclical interest in photography that lies dormant for thirty years, then re-erupts in a flurry of excitement for a few years, a behaviour pattern rather like that of a hyperkinetic child discovering a new toy.

One must consider this in the perspective of what other toys were lying about the art world in 1970. In fact there were surprisingly few. As in every decade since Dadaism the artistic and critical vanguard in the 1960s were cheerfully heralding the 'death of Art'. Oddly enough, in a very small way, and for a very brief period of time, their jeremiad was correct. Which is not to deny that in 1970 there were scores of significant artists producing work of enduring interest and worth. Merely that, by 1972 at the very latest, most of the major movements that had emerged in the previous decade – Minimalism, Post-Painterly Abstraction, Process Art, Earth Art, Linguistic Conceptualism, to name a few – had plateaued, insofar as their major issues had already been announced, major players already identified, and major works already made and entered in the culture. There was relatively little to see that one did not already know something about, and little visible on the horizons of painting, sculpture or conceptualism promised to be as interesting as the work that proceeded them.

The few remaining unexploited areas were video (with artists' films), performance, and photography. Laurie Anderson notwithstanding, the audience for performance, though passionate, is usually small. That left video artists' films and photography. Most knowledgeable observers favoured the former, heedless of the inherent suspicion attending 'real-time' art works and heedless as well of the notion that though the vanguard audience's masochism is great, it is not infinite. The knowledgeable observers were wrong, not for the first time.

Many of the reasons for photography's art-world ascendance were shameful, or irrelevant. As the acerbic H. L. Mencken observed fifty years ago, no one ever went broke underestimating the taste of the American public. Mencken's spiritual descendant, Tom Wolfe, further noted in his broadside *The Painted Word*, that the American art audience, even at its most sophisticated levels, hankers deep down for imagistic art; if possible, figurative art, an art with recognizable forms and an anecdotal degree. Most photographs automatically satisfy this in some degree. While abstraction held the high ground in American painting and sculpture since 1945, it has remained, for a number of reasons, only a factional style in American photography. Critics, most of whom if trained at all are trained as writers, also prefer artwork that yields up to literary interpretations. It is, after all, easier to write about a Diego Rivera painting, or a Cartier-Bresson photograph, than it is to confront the obdurate materiality of, for instance, a Carl Andre sculpture.

Thus photography inherited some of that portion of the American art audience too intellectually torpid to understand, much less take interest in, the kinds of issues raised by the best American art of the 1960s. Photography appeared more easily accessible. Which it is, though only superficially. The fact that the most intelligent photographic works hold a range of problematic issues as demanding as those raised by any other art of major ambition, either came as a rude shock to this segment of photography's public, or else was overlooked by it altogether.

Another less than noble reason why photographs, rather than video or performance art, dominated the stage in the 1970 was because photographs, unprepossessing though they may be, nevertheless can be shown as tangible objects in a way that video and performance cannot. Not only are photographs a tangible commodity, but, judging from auction prices during the 1970s, a vastly underpriced one at the start of the decade. More than one observer has conjectured that before 1970 it would probably have been possible to purchase every twentieth-century photograph in the Museum of Modern Art's exemplary *Masters of Photography* installation for less than the price of one major contemporary painting. This inequity was more than redressed by the early 1980s when a Los Angeles television producer allegedly paid over $70,000 for an uneditioned mural-sized print of Ansel Adam's celebrated *Moonrise Over Hernandez, New Mexico.*

Another development in American photography during the 1970s was the unprecedented quantity and quality of photographers' and artists' publications, some in the form of portfolios or original prints, some in the traditional form of a monograph by an established publishing house, but most often, in the form of inexpensively printed, self-published 'artist's bookworks' that dealt with a single subject or theme. A number of external circumstances contributed to help make this a possibility for photographers in the 1970s: support from the ubiquitous NEA; improvements in the technology of photographic reproduction; the formation of book distributors and retailers specialized in artists' books; and the aforementioned college-age public, which was interested in photography but whose affluence extended to posters and books rather than to original prints. Most important, though, was that this form of organizing and disseminating photographic images responded to a concern generated in photography during the 1970s.

Long constrained by the preciosity of the 'master' print and dismayed by the informational limitations of the single image, many photographers chose to work in groups of serial or sequential images, often narrative but many times not. These photographers came to regard the single print as an element of a larger entity: the series, sequence or group, which was, rather than the individual photography, the indivisible unit. Further, many of these photographers were coming to resent the reduction of the photograph to commodity status, costly and rare, and preferred to make their ideas and images available at a low cost to the widest possible audience. At the same time they were wary of the magazine as a means of dissemination, being all too aware of the dubious role played by editors in 'mediating' the photographers' intentions. The self-published book seemed an appropriate vehicle.

Among the earliest 'book works' was the witty and visually intelligent *Twenty-Six Gasoline Stations*, published by Ed Ruscha in 1962. The modest little paperbound book contained exactly twenty-six photographs of gasoline stations, fulfilling to the letter the claim of its title. Though Ruscha did not, and does not consider himself a photographer as such, this little book, and others by him that followed, had an enormous impact on photography. Far from being stigmatized as 'vanity' books, artists' and photographers' books increasingly came to be seen as the most vital and interesting area of art publishing, so much so as to rob the high-ticket productions of established publishers of their traditional prestige. It was generally understood that any innovative, serious photography could only be produced through some form of self-publication, leaving the large commercially houses as the dinosaurs of the field, able only to produce safe crowd-pleasers: Ansel Adams monographs, or the celebrity photos of a Linda McCartney.

The most interesting publications during the 1970s were usually done outside commercial channels, as bound portfolios of original prints, self-published efforts, very small presses, such as Lustrum, university presses, or not-for-profit publishing houses, most notably Aperture. The most interesting of these publications were the thematic works such as Robert Adams' *The New West* (1974), *Denver* (1977), and *From The Missouri West* (1980); Larry Clark's genuinely shocking *Tulsa* (1971); Linda Connor's *Solos* (1979); Robert Cumming's *Picture Fictions* (1973) and *The*

Weight Of Franchise Meat (1971); William Eggleston's *Election Eve* (1976), an epic portfolio of 100 images; Lee Friedlander's classics *Self-Portrait* (1970) and *The American Monument* (1976); Ralph Gibson's *The Somnambulist* (1970), which suggested new possibilities of sequencing; John Gossage's *Gardens* (1978), a bound book of original prints with a text selected by Walter Hopps; Chauncey Hare's *Interior America* (1978); and Mike Mandel and Larry Sultan's remarkable *Evidence* (1977), to name a few of the best. The Age of Mechanical Reproduction had begun to filter down to the working photographer.

Perhaps the last institution to be mentioned might be the critical press, if only because it disappointed so many of the expectations it raised. One of the hopes for photography in the 1970s was that it would attract the critical attention of leading writers and thinkers outside the photographic community. This much at least was fulfilled: photography exerted a fascination for art writers who had made substantial reputations for their critical views on the other plastic arts. However, almost without exception they failed to come to terms with photography in any but the most superficial way. The astuteness that had gained them such success in other areas was abandoned as they became seduced by the most trivial instances and trivial issues in photography. Few retired from the field with their reputations untarnished; many were in tatters.

The most egregious example was Susan Sontag's *On Photography*, an edited anthology of articles written for the *New York Review of Books* in the early 1970s.[4] One critic was unkind enough to remark that since Sontag could no longer think nor write she should consider not publishing the results of her losing struggle. Though perhaps too harsh a judgment, there is little doubt that *On Photography*, with its unsupported assertions, poorly reasoned arguments, and internal contradictions, is not Sontag's finest work. Nevertheless the book became the nearest thing to a bestseller that photographic criticism had yet enjoyed, and most right-thinking American readers believed that they could learn everything necessary about photography, both as a cultural artefact and as a form of aberrant behaviour, in the pages of this simplistic book.

By the late 1970s the only predictably serious source of critical writing about photographs came from the Marxist point of view. To their credit, Marxist critics were among the few who addressed photography in terms of social issues, who advertised their biases, and campaigned actively for what little of the photographic they found that met their ideological requirements. To their discredit they, with few exceptions (one thinks here of the often droll Alan Sekula), expressed their convictions in a hectoring, turgid prose, so riddled with appropriated jargon as to be virtually unreadable to any but the initiated. Some found it ironic that the last convincing humanist philosophy would present itself in such élitist trappings; others found the disengagement of theory from practice, and the emphasis on theory, transparently self-serving.

Nevertheless, the Marxists represented the only body of photographic criticism taking a position of militant advocacy during the 1970s. This seemed to result from a view that most non-Marxist critics took of their own role: they perceived their first duty as taking a censorious position toward work which they deemed inadequate, rather than articulating and supporting the aesthetic of works in which they believed. Such a position may be adequate for newspaper writing but it parts company with the best of twentieth-century art criticism, from Apollinaire to Greenberg, which saw its role as defining and advancing a particular position in the arts, and calling attention to artists and works that advanced that position in practice.

It would be unwise to overlook the terrible creative and destructive energies in American society, how they were brought to bear upon photography in the 1970s, and how these energies transformed the material and philosophical circumstances of American photography. It would be equally unwise to forget that had there not existed a large, vital body of photographic practice in America, the support systems would have counted for little. One could also argue that it was the claims of American photography that brought the support systems into being. Both views are tendentious. In fact the interaction between the large and committed body of photographic practice and existing institutions brought lasting changes to both.

Few would dispute the insularity of serious photography in America prior to the 1970s, although there is disagreement about whether this isolation was benign or stultifying. Photographer Robert Fichter compared photography with a Greek island, in the best sense; a sunny, carefree place in the mind where visitors were welcome to bask.[5] A less generous observer might have characterized it differently: as a mixture of a Rotary meeting and a Klan gathering, replete with secret handshakes, arcane shibboleths, and a fiercely defensive assertion of its parochial values in the face of a harsh and indifferent world. Photography's entrance into the mainstream of American culture changed all of that, the good and the bad, permanently. Henceforth photographic practice and theory would be held to the same standards used to assess other ambitious contemporary art, and a number of practices and attitudes from the 1950s and 60s would no longer play. Traditional photographers could no longer have the luxury of disguising the bankruptcy of their vision behind technically 'perfect' prints and pseudo-spiritual utterances; soi disant 'experimental' photographers could no longer pretend that Robert Rauschenberg had not gotten there first, and done it better, ten years before. Those stables, and others, were being swept, and those who were brushed aside complained that photography had lost its innocence.

Much of the American photography of the 1970s seems curiously affectless and divorced from the political, social, and interpersonal issues that surfaced during the decade. If it is so, it is less the blame of uncaring photographers than of those same photographers' chastened view of the powers of their medium. During the 1950s and 60s 'concerned' photography was perceived, at least by its makers, as a form of activism. By the 1970s it became clear to more thoughtful photographers that is was, in truth, the antithesis of effective social involvement: a form of elitist play-acting, morally satisfying to the player, but without serious political or social consequence. If one wished to influence social or political issues, then images were no substitute for direct political struggle. Photography's value lies elsewhere: in describing the surfaces of the phenomenal world in a manner unique to itself; hoping, at best, to contribute a precise, if necessarily limited, understanding of the objects and events in front of the lens, and some insight into the mind behind it.

These attitudes did not begin, nor have they ended with the 1970s. Many of the dominant attitudes, issue, styles and personalities of that decade have their origins in the 1960s and, by extension, in the entire history of photography. For those issues inherited from the near past, the 1970s were a culmination and a fulfillment: to such a degree that they could be said to belong to the 1970s, as much as to any other decade.

In the late 1960s three extremely influential exhibitions introduced what would become the mainstream issue in American photographic work throughout the 1970s. These exhibitions were *Toward a Social Landscape*, *Twelve Photographers of the American Social Landscape* and *The New Documents*. Two of the three exhibitions incorporated in their title the term 'Social Landscape', a phrase coined by Lee Friedlander some time earlier. Friedlander, along with his two colleagues Diane Arbus and Garry Winogrand, formed the nucleus of 'Social Landscape' photography.

It was a useful term to embrace the cool, laconic, post-Pop look of much of the best of contemporary American photographs in the 1960s and 70s. Its subject was an America no longer postwar, and it's hidden agenda a redefinition of photographic formalism. Formalism is usually taken in photography in its smaller sense: the orderly and considered distribution of elements within the frame to achieve a 'pleasing' arrangement of shapes, tones, etc. With the works of Friedlander and Winogrand, formalism in photography came to take on the broader definition that critics such as Greenberg and Fried has assigned to it in painting: the investigation of the material and historic possibilities of a medium, using that medium as the tool of investigation. In other words, a definition, *in practice*, of the extreme frontiers of what may be deemed as 'photographic' seeing. This, and not the adoption of the snapshot as a vernacular model, as Janet Malcolm suggested, is the way in which photography became 'Modernist.'[6]

'Social Landscape' had another antecedent than the snapshot: the work of Walker Evans. For a great number of American photographers he is what Cartier-Bresson is to the French: an artist with an inexhaustible heritage. Be this true or false, Evans' ironic, dialectical images informed much of the sensibility of the 'Social Landscape' photographers. Evans' irony was more than a detached superiority, it was, at its best, a form of reserved judgment, an appropriate stance from which to view a society whose ideals, fortunes, and individuals are in constant flux, and this lesson was not wasted on the generation of photographers who came to artistic maturity in the 1960s and 70s.

In very different ways the three leading photographers of 'Social Landscape' challenged the prevailing ideas of what photographs must look like. Diane Arbus' artless, straightforward portraits resemble nothing more than fashion portraiture gone horribly wrong. Photographing the dark underside of American society, Arbus found horror and desolation not only in the most freakish of her subjects but, more eloquently, in the faces, postures, and costumes of 'normal', average Americans. No American photographer had ever taken such a relentless, surgical look at what lay beneath the surface of American society. Her closest counterpart might be the writer William Burroughs, whose *Naked Lunch* shared many of the elements of Arbus' sensibility.

Arbus' photographs posed troublesome ethical questions, about her as a photographer, and about ourselves as viewers. Did her work exceed the limits of her subjects' 'informed consent'? And how much are we, seduced by her vision, implicated with her – and with the depravity she so often photographs? For, if Arbus' photographs are sensational, voyeuristic, and exploitative, they are also undeniably compelling for reasons that seem to transcend, or at least short-circuit, our moral responses. There has never been anyone quite like Arbus in the history of American photography and, despite her suicide in 1971, her presence was felt throughout much of the decade of the 1970s.

Garry Winogrand's photographs are possibly the highest expression of the phenomenal approach to photography in our time. His work illustrates, explains and fulfils his much quoted aphorism that he photographed in order to see what things would look like in photographs. He was a gifted and often scathing caricaturist, the American Daumier; and in their formal organization Winogrand's images pushed at the boundaries of photography *vérité*.

Taking nothing from the contributions of his contemporaries, Lee Friedlander stands out as the colossus whose work dominated American photography in the period 1967-80 and beyond. He is the only American photographer working whose images have assured him a place of honour among the photographers he admires: Atget, Evans, Cartier-Bresson, and Frank. His crowded, tense and often humorous images, and skein-like interlocking of pictorial elements were so complex, and so thoroughly defied traditional notions of photographic composition, that they were, literally, incomprehensible to many upon initial viewing, and were interpreted by some as metaphors for the obdurate chaos that is modern life. In retrospect that seems naïve. As Jonathan Green observed, for all their apparent disorder the images have a sophisticated and compelling logic, not unlike that of a Rauschenberg assemblage.[7] Like Rauschenberg, who wished to work in the area 'between art and Life,' Friedlander's seemingly haphazard compositions allowed his viewers to ponder the dialectic of curiously opposed objects and events that meet within his photographs much as they meet in out everyday vision. Friedlander has modified his strategies over the years, encompassing within his photographs a far wider variety of subjects and situations than any photographer working today.

But if a movement is to be worthy of a name, its vitality must be tested not only by the strength of its progenitors but by the strength of succeeding generations of workers as well. And it is against this critical test the 'Social Landscape' proved so durable, attracting, for a period, a group of photographers as interesting and diverse as Mark Cohen, Bill Dane, William Eggleston, Anthony Hernandez, Tod Papageorge, and Henry Wessel, Jr. Many of these photographers have found their mature expression in styles widely divergent from the 'Social Landscape' aesthetic, others have extended the idiom and forged from it an instrument of strong personal expression. But it touches, at one time or another, all of these prominent photographers of the 1970s and many made their work in that style.

Another powerful hold over from the 1960s was the increased use of photographs by artists not usually thought of as photographers. At first these works surfaced as documentation of body art, earth-works and performance pieces; but by the mid-1960s artists such as Jan Dibbets, Douglas Huebler and Bruce Nauman were producing conceptual pieces in photography that could, in fact, only be executed as photographs. The 1970s saw an acceleration of the use of photographs in conceptual art, and by the mid-1970s artists, such as John Baldessari, Lucas Samaras, and William Wegman, not usually considered as photographers, were producing bodies of work that were decidedly photographic, both in concerns and in materials. The only argument for creating a distinction between these photographs and 'photography' was the price gradient between photographs and other mediums, a powerful enough argument in a capitalist society.

Muddying the waters further were a number of persons, generally thought to be primarily photographers, such as Thomas Barrow, Michael Bishop, Robert Cumming, Jan Groover, Ken Josephson, Ray Metzker, and Eve Sonneman, whose work addressed a broad sweep of issues previously considered the domain of other visual arts.

One further development of this trend was a heightened interest on the part of late-1970s American photographers in working in the controllable environment of the studio rather than the haphazard out-of-doors. In the studio, the photographer could direct, exactly and specifically, the content of his or her images, in a way common to other artists, and common to commercial photographers, but unusual in art photography. By changing from an analytic to a synthetic mode, photographers could lay to rest the last doubts regarding the issues of intentionality in their work. One thinks here of the works of JoAnn Callis, Barbara Kasten, Olivia Parker, and Sandy Skoglund. And especially one thinks of Cindy Sherman, whose enormously popular self-portraits utterly parted company with the 'still-life' look of so much made-in-studio work of the 1970s and resonate with associations of media imagery, autobiography, performance art, feminist role-investigations, and, in an oddly unsentimental sense, nostalgia.

The third, and less pervasive interest inherited from the 1960s that was to find its fulfillment in the years 1970-80 was mixed-media photography. It was a genuine attempt to take photography beyond the physical limitations of the unaltered photographic print and enhance it with the plasticity, objecthood, and visual surface of the other graphic arts. This work failed to gain wide acceptance outside the academic world for two reasons: first, few photographers working in this vein were able to transcend their indebtedness to Robert Rauschenberg's late 1950s work and second, the complexity of facture usually took precedence over the nominal content of the work, reducing photography from a relatively simple art to an extremely demanding craft. An exception should be made here for the work of Robert Heinecken during this period whose best efforts escape self-conscious facture and convey wit, intelligence, sexuality and rage. Two movements, or trends, seem to belong exclusively to the 1970s, the first, 'New Topographics' (after an exhibition in 1975 of that name), the second, what one might call, for want of a better phrase, 'The Rush to Color.'

'New Topographics' offered a radically reductive view of the American environment. Where those images that could be gathered under the rubric of 'Social Landscape' had the appearance of candour and immediacy, taking as they had Robert Frank as their mentor and the snapshot as their vernacular model, Topographic photographers opted to a chiller vision, arid and dispassionate. Their mentor was Timothy O'Sullivan and their vernacular model the commercial real-estate photograph. One useful description of the working ideology was given by photographer Joe Deal in the *New Topographics* catalog, "In making these photographs I attempted to make a series of images in which one image is equal in weight or appearance to another. Many of the conscious decisions made while the series was evolving has to do with denying the uniqueness in the subject matter in one exposure as opposed to another in the belief that the most extraordinary image might be the most prosaic."[8]

The conscious attempt to, if not eliminate, at least minimalize the appearance of 'style' informed this approach to photography, as did the programmatic rejection of most of the elements and devices traditionally employed to make the world seem 'interesting' in photographs. These choices alone might explain why *New Topographics* work so alienated photographic audiences, defeating as it did the very expectations that they had been taught to bring to photographs.

This approach, unyielding as it may appear, was arrived at through more than sheer perversity. More positive reasons exist for the emergence of this style at this particular historical moment. As Barbara Rose observed, in a culture lacking a direct link with the mythologies of the classical world, an established church that encouraged religious art, or a monarchy to define the pinnacles of its social order, American art has traditionally found its most elevated subject matter in the natural landscape, often endowing it with qualities that transcend its literal appearance. [9]

Needless to say, this has been even truer of photography in America, where landscape has been among its most important and enduring subjects. Unfortunately, by the late 1960s there was no convincing school of landscape photography in America. The vital West Coast School, founded by Edward Weston, had entered its late-mannerism phrase, typically producing oversized, overworked calendar pictures of mountains and black skies, while the Equivalent, with its roots in Stieglitz and carried through by Minor White, has degenerated into self-indulgent mystification.

Redeeming the American landscape for photography seemed a worthy task and more difficult than one might imagine. The present generation of Americans, for the most part, never experienced the landscape without experiencing its counterface, industrialism, and it seemed likely than without this dialectic the entire notion of 'pre' landscape might seem so estranged from ordinary reality as to appear escapist and sentimental. In this awareness topographic photographers surveyed the 'new' American landscape, attempting to see it whole and see it clear; motorways, shopping centres, housing tracts and all of the other elements that inform our perception of a landscape neither wholly natural nor wholly an agglomeration of industrial artefacts, the 'middle landscape' of late industrial pastoralism. This, even more than the heightened degree of traditional American photographic irony, was the vision that animated topographic photography in America during the last decade.

During the latter half of the 1970s American photography was overshadowed by one pervasive pseudo-issue, The Rush to Color, which blurred many of the existing lines demarcating areas of photographic practice and, in the end, cast a treacly pall over the entire enterprise. Unlike most of the trends operating in the 1970s, which had diverse and arguable beginnings, the Rush to Color began on 25 May 1976. On that date that Museum of Modern Art, New York, opened an exhibition of seventy-five dye-transfer color prints by contemporary Memphis photographer William Eggleston, accompanied by the publication of a book, William Eggleston's *Guide*, the first exclusively color monograph published by the Museum. Two months after the closing of the Eggleston exhibition the Museum opened its second one-person show of work by the contemporary color photographer, Stephen Shore.[10] MoMA, arguably the most prestigious single institution dealing with photography in America, had placed its imprimatur on color photography.

MoMA could hardly be faulted for its choices, however controversial they were at the time. Both Eggleston and Shore were and are photographers of exceptional talent and integrity, and cannot be held answerable for the flood of ingratiating rubbish that followed them into the museums and gallery any more than the QEII can be taken to task for the flotsam that accumulates in her wake. Despite radical differences in style, technique, and temperament, Eggleston and Shore shared a commitment to the use of color as a descriptive, as opposed to decorative, element in their photographs. They were among the last to do so and by the end of the decade it seemed as though their work, almost solely, redeemed the entire shallow, dismal affair that was America's flirtation with photographic color.

The dominant, or at least prevalent, body of color photographs that one saw at the shank of the seventies was vapid, overscaled, coffee-table art, the end-product of photography's first demand/supply style of photography: Soft Contemporary, user-friendly pap devoid of any content save color and any ideology save pettiness. The nearest parallel in recent history is with the second-generation color painters of the early 1970s, stain-painting and the like. The lesson of this style was to demonstrate that even painting, with its inherent physicality, plasticity, greater scale, and, of course, historical momentum, could not build a workable aesthetic upon color alone. And what was not possible for painting in the early 1970s was even less possible for photography at the close of the decade. Photography had made its blood sacrifice to the twin altars of interior decoration and corporate collecting, and in so doing strained the credulity of its audience, perhaps the most credulous on earth.

Photography's career in the mainstream of America's art

world was meteoric, coming and going. Summoned into the limelight in the early 1970s photography was dismissed with equal suddenness in favour of Neo-Expressionist painting, a largely European style that captured the attention of the American art world in 1980 and holds it still. In the public sector Reagonomics dictated the rationale for sweeping reductions in public arts funding, a decision that one cannot help suspect was based as much on ideological as fiscal motives. Reflecting the general hardening of attitudes in the late 1970s and 80s, student enrolment in art and photography courses stabilized and began to diminish. Economics, as well as hubris and poor business sense closed a number of the photographic galleries that had opened in the 1970s and reduced others to a skeletal version of their former selves. Most of the other art galleries that adopted photography into their programme in the 1970s continue to maintain their commitment to the medium, although not at the frenetic pace of eight years ago. If we have not seen – by any means – the end of photography in the art world, we have seen its limits. Nothing, as the cliché tells us, lasts forever.

On the positive side, nearly all of the photographers represented in this section are alive and working, and many are producing the most significant work of their careers. A new generation of color photographers has emerged, young enough to see color as simply another aspect of the medium rather than an issue apart or an ornament, and old enough to hold no extravagant hopes for popularity. At least two commercial galleries have opened in New York since 1980 with a commitment to photographic works: Pace MacGill which exhibits photography exclusively and the influential Metro Pictures which has exhibited the works of such post-modernists as Louise Lawler, Richard Prince, and Cindy Sherman. If photography has lost editorial space in the leading art journals, we may be consoled that Afterimage (from the Visual Studies Workshop), like the poor of the Bible, is always with us. A number of attitudes, issues, and personalities had to be cast aside when photography made its move upward in the world, and even more as it fell from grace. Yet it seems doubtful, in retrospect, if so many of those triaged photographers' ideas and works will be so sorely missed after all.

Consistent with the Puritanical strain of American thought that views the world and all its contents as temptations placed before us to test our souls, one might view the situation of American photography during the 1970s as such a test. Having survived for so long in obscurity and privation, could the corpus of American photography endure success, even popularity, as well? The answer, from the perspective of the mid-1980s is yes, after a fashion. If our present decade seems less favourable to the enterprise of photography generally, it seems significantly more favourable to certain photography. This decade has proved more discriminating than the last; it could hardly be otherwise. And, if that is not enough, there is a final consoling thought: perhaps Marvin Heiferman was correct, that America's interest in photography is cyclical, and in another thirty years the love affair between America and her photography will blossom once more. Photography will be brought from the shelf and, once again, made much over. And those of us who live long enough can have the 1970s all over again.

[1] Editor's note: The former image is "Raising the Flag on Iwo Jima" taken by Joe Rosenthal on February 23, 1945, which first appeared in *Life* on March 26, 1945. The latter image was published as the cover photograph for *Newsweek* on April 21, 1975.

[2] See Bill Jay, "Photography in America," *British Journal of Photography*, 11-18 July 1980.

[3] John Szarkowski, *Mirrors and Windows: American Photography Since 1960* (New York: Museum of Modern Art, 1978).

[4] Susan Sontag, *On Photography* (New York: Farrar, Strauss, and Giroux, 1977).

[5] Quoted in Louise Katzman, *Photography in California, 1945-80* (New York: Hudson Hills, 1984).

[6] See Janet Malcolm, *Diana & Nikon: Essays on the Aesthetic of Photography* (New York: David R. Godine: 1980). The book collects several essays Malcolm wrote on photography for *The New Yorker* in the 1970s.

[7] Jonathan Green, *American Photography, A Critical History 1945 to present* (New York: Harry N. Abrams, 1984).

[8] William Jenkins, *New Topographics: Photography of a Man-Altered Landscape* (Rochester: International Museum of Photography at George Eastman House, 1975).

[9] Barbara Rose, *American Painting: The Twentieth Century* (Geneva: Skira, 1969).

[10] For practical purposes I am ignoring an earlier Helen Levitt exhibition from 1974 based on projected transparencies.

Text originally appeared in *American Images: Photography 1945-1980*, ed. Peter Turner (London: Barbican Art Gallery / Penguin Books, 1985).

Notes on *Waffenruhe*

A republic of images. It is early March 1988 and everyone who has ever had the intention to photograph Berlin has probably done this by now. In the last seven or eight years, the city has become established as a place for serious photographic work and it has attracted numerous interesting artists from Germany and abroad. And for a good reason: Apart from New York and its legend of ambition and success endlessly reproducing itself, Berlin is the last mythic city of the occident. If Berlin had not already existed, Calvino would have invented it.

London, Paris, Rome, have a history, but Berlin has a past. It is the Sodom of our century, destroyed for its sins and left like that as a dark memorial. Since the 1920s, Berlin has been a city approached through images: Döblin, Pabst, Isherwood; the vicious shrine of Nazism; the Year Zero; the Airlift, John Kennedy and the spies who came from the cold; the generation of '68, the stylized desperation of the punk underground and angles you can touch, these are some of the images making the myth. Myths, however, do not only lend events a human dimension, they are also manufactured to mystify experiences. Mythic images are perhaps those you have to be most suspicious of. Yet the idea of a post-apocalyptic city captivates the contemporary spirit and images of it spring like mushrooms again. Berlin will soon be as flooded with pictures as New York and Paris and the images of the city will have lost all their power, except to reflect and remind of each other.

The best photographer of Wartenburgstraße. Michael Schmidt was born in Berlin in 1945 and has photographed the city for nearly twenty years. Schmidt's work maintains a dialectic relation to Berlin; his photographs and the city explain each other. Of the thousand pictures populating Berlin, many of the most memorable are those by Schmidt. Schmidt continues to photograph Berlin and the viewer continues to see Berlin with his eyes. But now something new happens: Photographer and viewer see Berlin as if it was for the first time.

Schmidt is an artist of protean intellectual energies. Furthermore, he is an artist of the fragment, of complexity, of contradiction. His work is consistent and versatile. In *Waffenruhe* he is also passionate, which makes this collection of photographs his most intense and poignant to date. Not only does this mean that Schmidt is a better artist now, but also that he has become an entirely different artist. He has – except for the most rudimentary – cut all ties with the traditional documentary style and replaced it by an aesthetic of immediate experience. There is no confusion, no hide and seek in *Waffenruhe.* Schmidt's work is full of self-confidence and authority now.

Questions of space and time. The protagonist of *Waffenruhe* is the Berlin Wall or more precisely the city limits and some of the things happening within them. A fifth of the photographs show the Wall; another fifth alludes to its presence; almost all imply its existence. The Wall is Berlin's dark symbol of itself, the most representative landmark of the city, a kind of sinister Eiffel Tower. However, as the Eiffel Tower somehow "naturalizes" Paris (Barthes), the Wall reinforces Berlin's artificiality and elusiveness.[1] The Wall is Europe's most atrocious landmark, yet it is also the one where use value and symbolic value are most closely linked. Michael Schmidt lives in Wartenburgstraße, near the Wall. Everyone lives more or less near the Wall in Berlin.

The photographs in *Waffenruhe* have probably been taken over the course of a year, maybe even several years, but with the exception of just a few pictures, they all convey the feeling of a certain specific season when a severe winter makes way for spring. This feeling stems from the iconography of the images, but it also is a quality of their color and temperature. Yet as these photographs are black and white and do not have a specific temperature, this is either a paradox or a misconception of the critic.

Non-light. It is noticeable that a considerable part of German art photography of the last twenty years, since the Bechers, that is, avoids the effects of direct lighting. This might be a reaction to the kitschy, garish light and shadow constructions of the time of the Bauhaus. But in this case, there might be an ambitious statement behind it: that German post-war photography is more conceptual and oriented more towards the Platonic spiritual heights where pure forms and entities reign over the false and transient world of appearances. Be it as it may, photographs in such dark, lightless tones always seem more serious, disciplined and, in a certain stereotypical sense, more German. Some of the images in *Waffenruhe* have this cerebral gray, but Schmidt turns this convention on its head. When Schmidt takes away the light from an image, there remains a kind of gray so absolute that it radiates perversely, an inversion of photographic beauty, but beautiful nonetheless.

If you have no chance, take it. It was by no means inevitable that German photography would attain the same maturity as German painting or film. Indeed, it was most doubtful. In the last two years, however, it has become apparent that German photography has reached a fully developed autonomous state. *Waffenruhe* is part of the evidence for it.

A Norwegian photographer friend of mine said *Waffenruhe* was the most important photobook by a contemporary European photographer. This is impossible to prove or disprove, but it is an opinion worth taking seriously. *Waffenruhe* does not resemble anything that preceded it. The most striking quality of the book is its intensity. Schmidt's images and their sequence have a rigor that makes them hard to look at and impossible to wipe off the table. In his earlier works Schmidt had documented the social artifacts of contemporary Berlin; with *Waffenruhe* he created an autonomous work, a new cultural artifact standing for itself, something whose existence changes the world it records. If we ask *Waffenruhe* the same question we asked Schmidt's earlier works: "Does Berlin really look like that?" The most appropriate answer would be: "Yes, it does now."

[1] Editor's note: On Roland Barthes and the naturalization of myth, see Roland Barthes, *Mythologies*, first English edition (New York: Farrar, Straus, and Giroux, 1972).

This text originally appeared in *Camera Austria*, German trans. W. Prantner, No. 26 (1988). Editor's note: The text is a review of Michael Schmidt, *Waffenruhe* (Berlin: Berlinische Galerie, Fotografische Sammlung, in association with Dirk Nishen Verlag, 1987).

The Deaths in Newport

In 1988 I was living in Milan, in my wife's house, witnessing and participating in the deterioration of my third marriage. We had moved to Milan from Paris that winter, giving up an apartment near Denfert-Rochereau that we had shared for two years. My wife had lived in Paris, off and on, since 1979 and loved the city. I detested Paris, or believed that I did. She hated Milan, where she had grown up, and felt that returning was an admission of defeat.

Reluctant to exchange Paris for Milan, she insisted that we try another city; her choice was Los Angeles where she had a number of friends and had visited often on architectural assignments. I had been raised in Southern California and I had many of the same feelings about LA that she did about Milan; there was a certain symmetry in the exchange. Los Angeles held none of the glamour for me that it did for her, but if I loathed LA at least I understood it only too well and felt an alienation different from that which I had experienced living as a foreigner in Paris. I found a position as Visiting Artist at a university there; we rented an apartment in Westwood. I reestablished contact with my analyst in Berkeley – by telephone – and I began to look for a project that would keep me in LA.

My wife had received an assignment from an Italian architecture magazine to photograph some of the new buildings at the University of California, Irvine and I went along for the ride. Newport Beach, adjacent to the Irvine campus, had been my hometown but I hadn't been back in years. I had spent a classically miserable youth there, and had never been especially eager to return.

After working part of the day at U.C.I. we drove to Newport Beach to see Chris Burden's exhibition at the Newport Harbor Art Museum.[1] Leaving the museum later I saw a notice of the museum's plans for a new building.

Although it had been easy enough for me to rationalize my distaste for my childhood home – Orange County, and Newport Beach, were synonymous with the politics of the crypto-fascist right – my problematic sprung from far more personal reasons.

One thing that was difficult to fault, though, was the Newport Harbor Art Museum, which had taken on the role of an excellent small contemporary art venue in recent years, under the leadership of Kevin Consey, the museum's ambitious director, and Paul Schimmel, a brilliant young curator from New York. Recently the museum had begun to monumentalize its ambitions for world-class status by initiating a program for a new building.

Toward this goal the Irvine Company, Orange County's largest landholder and development company, had donated twelve acres of land at the corner of the Pacific Coast Highway and MacArthur Boulevard, the primary access street to the John Wayne International Airport and the San Diego, Newport and Corona del Mar freeways.

The museum sponsored an international architectural competition for the 50 million dollar building project. The winning architect was Genoa-based Renzo Piano, whose previous museum designs included the Centre Pompidou in Paris (with Richard Rogers) and the de Menil Museum in Houston, thought by many to be the most intelligent museum design built in the past decade.

It had become customary to create a photographic document of the building of major cultural centers – both the Getty Museum and LAMOCA had commissioned an art photographer to make a project, with broad frontiers of what that project may be, as a "site document." Such was the work I did then, or had done in the past. I proposed myself to the museum as the author of the site documentation project. My credentials were rather good for this, as the museum already owned a major work of mine which they had recently exhibited, and I played strongly on the home-boy advantage: I had been born and raised eight blocks from the proposed building site.

My offer was received with interest by the museum and I was asked to develop and submit a specific proposal for the project, with informal assurances that anything within reason would probably be accepted and funded. I spent a day walking the site with the director, and looking at Piano's model and floor plans.

What I didn't recognize at the time was that my interests had changed. I had photographed construction/destruction sites since 1970, had published two lengthy books on the subject and had done a number of smaller projects and commissions dealing with the transitional landscape. I had arrived at a point where I couldn't accept to do this same work for another two years. I felt that there was nothing more that I could learn from this practice and I wanted to move on to make new work. It seemed to me that if I took the idea of site less literally, perhaps to include the town, it would offer more possibilities.

My memories of Corona del Mar were quite black and I was surprised at what I found on my return. Of course, everything was smaller, and nearer, than I had remembered. Long journeys, solitary adventures, in fact took place within a few blocks, and a wild canyon near my parents' house was in fact only a largish gully.

Walking around Corona del Mar for the first time since junior high school, I had certain expectations. I thought that long suppressed childhood memories would flood back, a dramatic recollection of a moment of abandonment and loss: a catharsis that would lead me out of my present crisis. I remembered Corona del Mar as bleak and empty as a Hopper painting but far more malign. I expected, hoped, that its present reality would resonate with my memories, that I would find a townscape redolent of evil. I was oddly disappointed, like a soldier returned to a distant battlefield and finding farms and houses and churches – or perhaps a motorway and factories. Corona del Mar was simply a more affluent version of what it had always been, a small, snobbish California beach town, like a dozen others on the coast.

Because I was so focused on my own past my mind drifted to the history of the town. Had anything ever happened here of note, something worth memorializing, something that could be grasped as emblematic of the place? A defining narrative? I went to the public library, adjacent to the museum and looked at fiches of old local newspapers dating from my childhood. As I went back closer to the date of my birth I discovered, or remembered, a story, which I had been told as a small child and had never completely forgotten.

A few minutes before midnight on March 15th, 1947, the *Mary E*, a 47-foot motor cruiser, exploded at her moorings in Newport Harbor killing Mr. Walter E. Overell, a 62-year-old Pasadena financier and his 57-year-old wife, Beulah.

The blast blew two holes in the hull of the boat, shattered decks and bulkheads, and was heard from over a mile away. The force of the explosion had shorn both of the victims' bodies of clothing. Overell's right leg had been shattered and a plank driven through his back; Beulah Overell's head had been crushed. The Overell's daughter, Beulah Louise, 17, and her fiancée, George "Bud" Gollum, 21, had escaped the blast by going ashore half an hour earlier for a late-night snack. When the couple returned a few minutes after the blast the Coast Guard, unable to guarantee the security of the *Mary E*, asked them to return ashore.

On the following Wednesday, March 19, Beulah Louise and Bud returned to Newport Beach to retrieve the family automobile from the police. "I'm glad you dropped in," Newport Beach Police Chief H.R Hodgkinson told them, "it saves me the trouble of going after you." Hodgkinson placed the couple under arrest on suspicion of murder.

Earlier that day Orange County Sheriff James Musick had announced his evidence to the press: 31 unexploded sticks of Trojan brand dynamite were found on board the *Mary E*, along with detonators, lengths of electrical wire and adhesive tape and an alarm clock rigged as a timing device, its hands stopped at 11:46 PM, the time of the explosion. The sheriff speculated that the explosive had been rigged by an amateur who had not realized that each dynamite stick required its individual blasting cap to explode. Had all of the sticks of dynamite exploded the blast would have totally destroyed the vessel and any evidence.

The legal process that followed was the longest criminal trial in American history until that time, and one of the most publicized. Beulah Louise Overell and George "Bud" Gollum became familiar fixtures in the Southern California press over the next six months. 1947 was the heyday of the detective story in print and the trial took place at the pinnacle of public interest in murder mysteries. When the prosecution took its case to the public, it inherited not only an audience but also a format: which is to say that whatever the factual pattern of the case may have been, the prosecution narrative was constructed as a simulacrum of a detective story.

The Overell trial was among the last spectacular murder trials of the age of print media, and the story was carried daily in the *Los Angeles Times*; while the more sensationalist Hearst-owned *The Los Angeles Examiner* devoted pages one and two, usually with a third page of photographs, and hired romance novelist Adela Rogers St. Johns to write the "personal" side of the star-crossed lovers' story. The story was carried in the *New York Times*, *Life* magazine, and scores of other general interest journals, and of course most of the sixty magazines of police and detective fact and fiction were published each month.

The press focused on three features of the story: the heinousness of the crime, the love story between Bud and Beulah, and the journalists' opportunity to give their readers a glimpse into the scandals of the rich.

The first point is evident: parricide is the ultimate violation of the social contract inside the family and without. It breaks the code and the silence of the family and is the domestic equivalent of regicide. Though uncommon, the crime of double parricide is not as rare as one might imagine: California has averaged three such cases each year for the past two decades.

Parricides generally have common features, which derive from the logic of the act: the parents, or parents, though reduced to victims, retain an enormous psychological power over their assailants. It is extremely uncommon for a child to confront a parent and dispatch them with a single fatal wound. Usually the crime takes the form of an ambush, the assailant strikes unexpectedly from hiding. Parricides are usually committed by multiple wounds, far in excess of what would be merely fatal: the victims are shot, or stabbed, of bludgeoned again and again, suggesting either an uncontrollable rage on the assailants part or a need to kill over and over to assure the victims' death. The Overell deaths had elements of this modus operandi, though these features of "the classic parricide" had not been identified at the time.

Beulah Louise Overell was a 17-year-old, described in the *Los Angeles Times* as "the beautiful blonde heiress." An only child, she lived with a relative near the University of Southern California campus where she majored in journalism. Classmates described her as stolid and undemonstrative.

Her fiancée, George "Bud" Gollum was 21 years old, 6'1" tall, 220 lb. and handsome in the style of the times. A returned Pacific War veteran, Gollum had received the Bronze Star for bravery during the battle of the Leyte Gulf, and was a pre-med student at Los Angeles City College. Gollum's family had been acquainted with the Overell family for many years and the relationship between Beulah and Bud had started with the Overell's suggestion that Beulah write to Bud while he was overseas.

The couple had announced their engagement and their wedding date had been set for April 30. The Overells were said to have reservations about the marriage because of Beulah Louise's youth, but claimed to like Gollum and had consented on the condition that both finish college. "We planned to get a house trailer and live in a central spot near the campuses," Beulah told reporters.

The value of the Overell's estate was estimated to be over $600,000, which in 1947 had the same buying power as $6,116,000 in 2011.

The coroner's autopsies (there were two, the second made

after the Overell's burial – a third disinterment was refused by the court) revealed multiple skull fractures, delivered by the same implement, but the coroner could not determine whether the fractures had been the cause of death, although they seemed to correspond with a ball-peen hammer found on board the *Mary E.* The autopsy report further stated that there was no water in the lungs of the victims indicating that they may have died prior to the sinking of the vessel. On March 26 the Grand Jury returned unanimous indictments of murder against the accused couple.

Newport Beach police Captain Harry Lace was the officer in charge of the investigation. I met him at his home in the summer of 1989; we spoke for over five hours, about the trial, about my father, about the history and political economics of pre-war California. Driving back to Santa Monica I recalled the epigraph to Pinter's *The Go-Between*: "The past is a foreign country: they do things differently there…."[2] Lace was in many ways unlike any cop I'd met before. Imperially thin, he had the quasi-military bearing assumed by American cops, but his mentality revealed more Jeffersonian idea of the relation of the state to its citizens. I asked if he believed that Beulah Louise and Gollum were guilty he replied that, of course he did; he had headed the investigation and believed that the evidence supported his claim. But, he added, it was right that they were not convicted, because the prosecution had so mishandled the case, especially the physical evidence that Beulah and Bud "deserved to go free." I had never before heard a policeman take the position that the legal rights of the defendant took precedence over the issue of factual guilt or innocence; I doubt if I will again.

Lace was over 70 years old when I met him. He had left the

Newport Beach Police in 1958 and was never implicated in the scandals of corruption and brutality and harassment that came to be their trademark after 1960.

On April 4th, California State Attorney General Fred Howser removed Orange County District Attorney Davis from the prosecution. Davis had been openly skeptical of the state's case from the outset and he had acquired a reputation in the Orange County courts for his leniency toward minors, and women, especially in capital cases. Other members of the prosecutorial team, notably Police Chief Hodgkinson of Newport Beach believed that Davis was fulfilling something less than his full duties in prosecuting this case, in which a female minor was charged with a capital crime.

Hodgkinson made his objections known in a letter to newly-elected California State Attorney General Fred Howser. Howser removed Davis and took over the prosecution himself, a prerogative of his office. It was generally speculated that Howser, in office just a few months, welcomed the opportunity to be credited with the prosecution of what was generally believed to be an open-and-shut, high-visibility case. It was further speculated that it was Howser who contacted Hodgkinson and sought his request for Davis' removal.

Howser named Eugene Williams as Special Prosecutor in the case. Williams had recently returned from the Tokyo War Crimes trials where he had successfully prosecuted Premier Tojo and other leaders of the Japanese wartime government. Beulah and Bud chose a defense team led by Santa Ana attorney Otto Jacobs, a former president of the California Bar Association, well-known and highly respected in the local courts as an honest but ruthless and clever litigator.

During their pre-trial incarceration Beulah and Bud exchanged clandestine love letters, passed through a jailer, who gave copies to the prosecutor, who then passed the letters along to *The Los Angeles Examiner*, in repayment of a political debt owed by Howser to Hearst.

The letters were in part sexually explicit, in part ludicrous, in another measure a romantic fantasy of jail escape, suicide threats (Beulah wrote that she would kill herself if Bud ever loved another woman), a suicide pact, and idyllic dreams of their future life together in a trailer. By the time the trial opened, the reading public had an inside view of Bud and Beulah's romance.

On May 26th the trial commenced in the Santa Ana Superior Court, Judge Kenneth E. Morrison presiding. The jury selection took three and one-half weeks with 567 prospective jurors interviewed before a jury of six men and six women acceptable to both the prosecution and the defense could be impaneled. Having exhausted the voters' rolls, Judge Morrison revived an old circuit-court law and sent bailiffs roaming the streets of Santa Ana rounding up random citizens to stand for jury selection. As though in complicity with the Hollywood version of such event, the late spring and early summer had an unprecedented heat wave, with record temperatures reported on nearly every day of the trial in the crowded courthouse.

In his opening argument Prosecutor Eugene Williams graphically outlined the elements of the prosecution case, concluding that, "The defendants enjoyed an illicit, perverted, sadistic sexual passion amounting to...frenzy. Lust, greed, frustration, these are the raw materials of which murders are made." The burden of the State's case was that Beulah and Bud had beaten the

Overell's to death and then planted explosives on the *Mary E* to destroy the evidence of the crime.

The couple's lawyer, Jacobs, entered two pleas: Not Guilty and Not Guilty By Reason of Insanity, an option in capital cases in California at that time, the second plea being a safeguard to be used in the punishment phase of the trial should the jury return a guilty verdict. It is interesting to speculate upon what basis Jacobs would have established his insanity plea. It has been common practice in murder trials in the last decade to portray the female defendant as an incest victim, driven to her crime by fear and rage. But, although Beulah Louise Overell had many similarities to the incest survivor profile, such charges were considered so scandalous in 1947 that it would have been counterproductive to pursue that strategy. The *omerta* of the family took precedence over the rights of an abused child, or spouse.

Proceedings were enlivened on June 25th by a bizarre story of an assault told by one of the jurors, Mrs. Uvon Putnam. On the previous evening an unidentified man "with dark hair" forced entry into her Balboa Island home, beat her, threatening her that, "This isn't all you'll get if you find them guilty." Mrs. Putnam could give no further clues to the identity of the man and the Newport Beach Police placed the matter under investigation. Defense counsel issued a statement vigorously denying any implication in the assault, suggesting that the attack might have been an attempt by the prosecution to discredit the defense.

A pivotal element in the prosecution case was to establish that the Overell's had been murdered hours before the explosion – beaten to death in cold blood by Gollum – and that the dynamite was planted to destroy the evidence of the murder and give the appearance of an accidental explosion. It was therefore imperative that the prosecution establish the time of death as prior to 11:45 PM. The prosecution opened its case with two forensic experts. My father was the first prosecution witness to testify; as the local mortician he received and embalmed the bodies of Mr. and Mrs. Overell immediately after their death. Described as a "square-cut man with silvering hair," the "dapper mortician" testified that he had received the bodies at Baltz Mortuary at 2:45 AM, March 16th, and immediately embalmed the bodies. He testified that he believed the bodies to have been dead for approximately six hours at the time he first saw them. He added that Mr. Overell's clothing "reeked of gasoline." Under cross-examination my father was asked what method he used to determine time of death. Rigor mortis, he replied, (a stiffening of the body tissues of the deceased, which starts between four and ten hours after death) a commonly used method at the time.

Defense counsel – correctly – criticized his methodology as inaccurate, unscientific and subject to so many variables to be hardly more than folk-medicine, and went on to point out – again correctly – that he was not a medical doctor and possessed none of the qualifications to make such an assertion. Nonetheless the press reports that the defense lawyers failed to shake him from his previous testimony. In this photograph, which appeared in *The Los Angeles Examiner*, there a number of features that I find curiously anachronistic. The double-breasted pin-stripe suit, and patterned necktie look oddly contemporary, which, due to the politics of fashion, they could easily be. The microphone has another, more sinister association: a few years later hundreds of public officials and private citizens were to be paraded before similar microphones admitting or denying their membership in the Communist Party, betraying, or refusing to betray their comrades. The man at the microphone would become the icon of the McCarthy Era, already starting. Only my father's physiognomy places him in his period; as is true with most of the people in these photographs. Somehow, people of this time – even stripped of identifying iconography – look different than we do, their faces as alien to us as the portraits of Renaissance princelings and banditti that fill the museums of Italy, or than the Protestant burghers of northern Europe, their spiritual ancestors. Few things seem as distant as the near past.

I am obsessed by one idea here: both my father and my mother were the products of broken homes, one-parent families in an epoch where this was the exception rather than the rule. They swore to each other, and to me, retrospectively, that their child would never spend a moment of his pre-school life away from one or the other parent. So: if my father's testimony was, as every fact leads us to believe, in his eyes his defining moment, it seems inconceivable that he would not wish his much-loved wife present to witness and share in his moment of glory. If that is true, and if the family legend passed on to me about their vow to never leave their child alone is also true, I can then believe that on June 21, 1947, I, 19 months old, was also present at the trial. Of course this precedes any memory of my own and there are no facts to corroborate or deny this hypothesis.

Far more damaging to the defense case was the testimony of Lawrence Mathes, chief resident surgeon of the Orange County Hospital and acting county coroner. He testified that the Overell's death was the result of multiple skull fractures that occurred before the explosion and identified a metal rod, approximately 8 cm in diameter as the probable murder weapon.

Following Mathes' testimony photographs of the deceased

were then presented to the court by the prosecution. Newport Beach police Captain Harry Lace remembers them as ghastly. The mutilation of the bodies was extensive, especially to that of Mr. Walter Overell, whose back was blown away from his neck to the base of his spine. One juror was taken away to vomit. Bud Golum glanced and looked away; Beulah stared at the photograph of her father for several minutes, expressionless.

Crowds continued to mob the courthouse, stampeding for seats at the spectacle. Microphones concealed in the courtroom and in the judge's chambers broadcast the trial – a first. On August 12, Millicent Naylor, a New Jersey secretary vacationing in Southern California, visited the trial on her way to the beach, wearing a one-piece bathing suit. She told reporters that she had come to see the show; news photographers reversed the spectacle and took "cheesecake" photos of Ms. Naylor as she was denied entrance by a stern and patriarchal bailiff – an image both in composition and narrative oddly reminiscent of a generic expulsion from the garden. Two of these photographs found their way into *Life* magazine.

Relying on the strength of its chief forensic witness Dr. Mathes, a mountain of circumstantial evidence and the emotional appeal of the jailhouse love letters the prosecution rested its case.

In a brief opening statement Defense Counsel Otto Jacobs asserted his version of the facts: Walter Overell, depressed by financial reverses, had asked Gollum to purchase the dynamite to use in a suicide attempt, the dynamite had exploded prematurely, and that the prosecution was motivated not by the desire to seek justice but by California State Attorney General Howser's political ambition.

In a bold opening move the defense called Attorney General

Howser to testify, asking him to disclose the political machinations involved in bringing the charges against the couple. Though he of course denied any such motives, Jacobs had succeeded in raising the question before the jury.

The defense's next move was equally audacious: Jacobs accused the state's chief forensic witness, the reputable Dr. Mathes, with perjury, and brought in its own experts to testify that the injuries suffered by the Overells were the result of ricocheting sticks of unexploded dynamite that flew about the boat's cabin at the time of the explosion.

On October 5th, after 19 weeks of trial and 6,000 pages of testimony, the jury announced a verdict of not guilty to the packed courtroom and the 3,000 visitors waiting outside. Among the hundreds of conflicting stories, charges, allegations, and lies generated during the trial, only one fact is clearly knowable – the legal innocence of the accused. Their factual guilt or innocence will remain a matter of speculation.

Bud and Beulah had become estranged during their incarceration. "There will be no marriage," Beulah told the press, refusing to pose with Bud for the news photographers. The story disappeared from the newspapers within two days.

Bud Gollum left California and married an exhibition motorcyclist from a circus. He had two other brushes with the law, the first for transporting a stolen car across a state line that earned him one year in a Georgia prison, and again, as a much older man, for the cultivation of marijuana on his property in northern California, where he currently resides, raising horses and managing a boat rental in Lake County. In telephone interviews with the press he maintains his innocence. If he is still alive he would be 75 years old.

As though a precursor to the Patty Hearst story, Beulah Louise, now rich, married a Los Angeles policeman, one of her jailers when she was transported outside of Orange County, and had one child. They divorced and she remarried, and moved to Las Vegas. She was found dead "by mischance" of acute alcoholism in her Las Vegas home in August 1965, with two empty vodka bottles and a loaded rifle at her side.

California State Attorney General Fred Howser ran for re-election in 1950. In the greatest Republican political sweep in California history, the Republican Party carried every office except that of Attorney General. Hauser, whose political misfortunes had begun with the Overell trial and were compounded by allegations of connections to Los Angeles mob boss Mickey Cohen, had not even made it to the general election, but had been defeated in the Republican primary by his Democratic opponent, Edmund G. "Pat" Brown.

The Newport Harbor Art Museum rejected my proposal for a work on the Overell story, for the surprising reason that – after 43 years – it would still be a sensitive issue. The director, Kevin Consey, resigned to take directorship of the Museum of Contemporary Art, Chicago. The curator, Paul Schimmel, resigned to become chief curator at the Los Angeles Museum of Contemporary Art. The new museum building by Piano was also rejected and Piano was dismissed as architect in favor of continuing the search for an architect who would design a more traditional building. Ultimately, the project was abandoned, or placed in limbo, by the economic crisis. My third wife and I separated a few months later and were divorced the following year.

Until his death in 1956, my father delighted in telling and retelling the story of the Overell deaths and his role in the trial.

In the 47 years since the Overell trial, Orange County has become the dystopic nightmare that its heredity and environment had destined it to be; it kept almost all of its old lower middle-class vices and had added the infirmities of wealth. The Orange County courthouse where the trial took place was demolished in the early 1960s to be replaced by an International-style tower designed by Richard Neutra. During the move from the old Courthouse to the new the transcripts of the Overell trial, including the wire recording of the entire process, were misplaced and today cannot be found.

Secondly, there is every reason to suspect that our memory of dreams is not only fragmentary but positively inaccurate and falsified. On one hand it may be doubted whether what we dreamt was really as disconnected and hazy as our recollection of it; and on the other hand it may also be doubted whether a dream was really as connected as it is in the account we give of it, whether in attempting to reproduce it we do not fill in what was never there, or what had been forgotten, with new and arbitrarily selected material, whether we do not add embellishments and trimmings and round it off so that there is no possibility of deciding what its original content may have been ....[3]

Dostoevsky's sympathy for the criminal is, in fact, boundless; it goes far beyond the pity which the unhappy wretch may claim, and reminds us of the "holy awe" with which epileptics and lunatics were regarded in the past. A criminal to him is almost a Redeemer, who has taken on himself the guilt, which must else have been borne by others. There is no longer any need for one to murder, since he has already murdered; and one must be grateful to him for, except for him, one would have been obliged oneself to murder ....[4]

[1] Editor's note: The exhibition was "Chris Burden: A Twenty Year Survey," Newport Harbor Art Museum, Newport Beach, CA, USA, 1988.
[2] *The Go-Between*, directed by Joseph Losey, screenplay Harold Pinter, 1970, United Kingdom. Pinter's screenplay is an adaptation of L.P. Hartley, *The Go-Between* (London: Hamish Hamilton, 1953).
[3] Sigmund Freud, *The Interpretation of Dreams*, trans. and ed. James Strachey (New York: Basic Books, 1955) 516.
[4] Sigmund Freud, "Dostoevsky and Parracide" (1928), trans. James Strachey, *The Standard Edition of the Complete Psychological Works of Sigmund Freud*, Vol. XXI (1927-1931) (New York: W.W. Norton & Co., 1976) 177.

This text originally appeared in Lewis Baltz, *The Deaths in Newport* [CD Rom] (Rotterdam: Paradox, 1995).

City Limits (Or Has This Been Used Before?)

The following text was delivered at a symposium, *The Fault Zone*, held in May 1992, at the Los Angeles Municipal Art Gallery, Barnsdall Park, organized by the Getty Center For the Humanities, on the occasion of Joe Deal's retrospective exhibition.

The day before I had been at Yale, as a visiting artist, reviewing the thesis projects of the graduating M.F.A. students. Or pretending to. Actually, I, and most of the faculty, spent the previous two days in a bar next to the arts building that had 24-hour CNN. We were watching Los Angeles burn. Los Angeles International Airport had closed certain approach patterns vulnerable to sniper fire and air traffic in and out of the city was pandemonium. Other cities were burning too. Rumors circulated that there had been gunfire on the New Haven line, and the trains were stopped; parts of Manhattan were riot zones; looting in Times Square; scattered fires in SoHo and Tribeca. (What if we were stranded in New Haven? What if New Haven blew up? We'd hole up in Yale's Arts and Leisure building: defensible architecture, a real fortress.)

Meanwhile, back on the West Coast, there were still scattered fires and looting despite the imposition of martial law and a sunset curfew a couple of days before. The Municipal Art Gallery afforded a privileged view of the destruction, punctuated by helicopters sweeps with searchlights and megaphones. Pure Coppola. The only people present at the symposium were the participants, their friends, and the Barnsdall staff. I counted 27 in all. The curfew was still in effect so we had to finish our business before nightfall. (In fact the curfew was winding down and might soon be called off. And middle-class white people driving home in good cars along the Sunset corridor weren't exactly the target of the militia. Nevertheless, I had the impression that no-one wanted to violate the curfew, less for fear of rioters or police than the desire to not be perceived as elitist scofflaws.)

This text, largely the part from Virilio, became the basis for the project that I made with the students at the Beaux-Arts, Paris, later in 1992.

At the beginning of the 1960s, with black ghettos rioting, the Mayor of Philadelphia announced: 'From here on in the frontiers of the State pass to the interior of the cities.' While this sentence translated the political reality for all Americans who were being discriminated against, it also pointed to a larger dimension…

Basically the American mayor's statement revealed a general phenomenon that was just beginning to hit the capital cities as well as the provincial towns and hamlets, the phenomenon of obligatory introversion in which the City sustained the first effects of a multinational economy modeled along the lines of industrial enterprises, a real urban redeployment, which soon contributed to the gutting of certain worker cities such as Liverpool and Sheffield in England, Detroit and St. Louis in the United States, Dortmund in West Germany, and all of this at the very moment in which other areas were being built up around tremendous international airports, a METROPLEX, a metropolitan complex such as Dallas/Fort Worth. Since the 70s and the beginnings of the world economic crisis the construction of these airports was further subjected to the imperatives of the defense against air pirates…

Construction no longer derived from traditional technical con-

straint. The plan had become a function of the risks of 'terrorist contamination' and the disposition of sites conceived of as sterile zones for departures and non-sterile zones for arrivals...

When the French built 'maximum-security cell blocks' they used the magnetized doorways that airports had had for years. Paradoxically the equipment that ensured maximum freedom in travel formed part of the core of penitentiary incarceration. At the same time, in a number of residential areas in the United States, security was maintained exclusively through closed circuit television hook-ups with a central police station ...."[1]

It is estimated that Southern California will lose 400,000 jobs in the aerospace industry between now and 1995. It is further estimated that 200,000 of those jobs will be replaced by lower paying "service industry" jobs, 40% of which will be in the areas of private security. Virilio continues:

"The representation of the modern city can no longer depend upon the ceremonial opening of gates, nor on the ritual processions and parades lining the streets with spectators. From here on urban architecture has to work with the opening of a new 'technological space-time'. In terms of access, telematics replaces the doorway. The sound of gates gives way to the clatter of data banks and the rites of passage of a technical culture whose progress is disguised by the immateriality of its parts and networks. [emphasis mine]

In this new perspective devoid of horizon, the city is entered not through a gate nor through an Arc de Triomphe *but rather through an electronic audience system...."*[2]

Presumably, it was from this text that Bernard Tschumi lifted his observation that the gates of the modern city were the metal detectors at the airport, which is to say that to be "in" the city means to be in the city's surveillance network, an idea carried to its extreme in Durrenmatt's provocative assertion of surveillance as a proof of existence, "I am because I am watched."

This idea of sociability posits a newer idea of the *polis* – the site of watching and being watched, the site where surveillance and spectacle (political theater) produce and consume each other: a site where surveillance is taken as proof, if not of existence, but of citizenship, while in fact being its opposite.

This "new" idea of urbanism shares its central feature with traditional urban deployments: the reification of power. Cities function and look as they do because their owners inscribe in them the narratives of control; and cities also look and work as they do because their inhabitants subvert the owners will. This is the simple political economy of urbanism; anything else is spectacle. (But, of course, some spectacles are more engaging than others.)

Los Angeles is the first modern city to declare itself as pure spectacle, and remains first in the industrialization of imagery, whose production, consumption and mythology functions as a substitute for what elsewhere is lived reality, a theme park with a live-in audience of twelve million and, for the moment, the world leader in the dematerialization of urban space into representational space. And how can one represent something that (always/already) exists in the condition of representation, an "emblem among emblems" as Calvino puts it?[3]

Debord offers an option, if not an encouraging one: the spectacle can be criticized (only) in the language of the spectacle.[4]

Brecht, writing of his life in the film industry, said much the same. "Each day," he wrote, "I go to the place where lies are bought and sold. Hopefully to join the sellers."[5]

The key to the image of the city, even a city of images, is to follow the etiology of desire. (In *Silence of the Lambs*, mass-murderer Hannibal Lector spoke clearly: we can only covet the things we see each day.) Images are the vectors of desire, the fuel and product of the "Desire-machine," whose successful functioning relies on the compulsion inherent in the panopticon: since everything can be seen, everything *must* be seen.

In Wim Wenders' film *Until The End of the World*, Max von Sydow plays a state-of-the-art Faust, whose device that brings sight to the blind and blinds the sighted, a larval form of virtual reality in whose thrall all desire is satisfied by images, a virtual end of desire, end of the world, the spectacle beyond which other spectacles are no longer needed. The heroine has entered this spectacular mode and is lost to our world. Her companion William Hurt asks himself, "How can I cure Claire of the disease of images?" But he receives no reply.

[1] Paul Virilio, "The Overexposed City," trans. Astrid Hustvedt (New York: Urzone, 1986). Originally published as "La ville surexposée," from *L'espace critique* (Paris: Christian Bourgeois, 1984).
[2] Ibid.
[3] Italo Calvino, *Invisible Cities* (1972), trans. William Weaver (New York: Harcourt, Brace, Jovanovich, 1978) 23.
[4] Guy Debord, *The Society of the Spectacle* (1967), trans. Fredy Perlman and Jon Supak (Detroit: Black & Red, 1970).
[5] Bertolt Brecht, "Hollywood," *Poems, 1913-1956*, eds. John Willett, Ralph Manheim (New York: Methuen, 1976) 382.

This text is a transcript of a paper delivered at the symposium *The Fault Zone*, organized by the Getty Center for the Humanities at the Los Angeles Municipal Art Gallery, Barnsdall Park, May 1992, on the occasion of Joe Deal's retrospective exhibition. Other panelists were Joe Deal, Kurt Forster, Frank Gehry, Marvin Heiferman, and Dennis Oppenheim.

Learning from Luxembourg

A former East German colleague celebrated his, and his country's, entrance into the free-market system by purchasing shares on the stock exchange. Visiting his broker one day he was astonished by the magnitude and speed of the markets and inquired if it wasn't all a bit dizzying, watching so much money changing. The broker corrected him: "The money never changes; only the owners change."

In Zurich there's a story that refuses to die: as you promenade along the Banhofstrasse the ill-gotten wealth of this century rests just beneath your feet. In catacomb-like vaults the great Swiss banking houses mingle the assets of Holocaust victims and Nazis, Mafiosi and deposed monarchs, petty dictators and cocaine lords, indistinguishably merged in bars of pure gold .999 fine. The story is probably apocryphal, but persists because it reaffirms an ancient and seductive image of tangible wealth, wealth as *materia*. Like *Goldfinger*, one could dream of touching it, stealing it. Wealth as wealth should be.

Wealth, as it really is, keeps moving around. Banking may be Switzerland's principal industry, but it's not its only one, and Switzerland, though small, is nonetheless a country, with the realities of global trade, unemployment, and immigration making its banking system increasingly vulnerable to international pressures. What capital markets demand now is a non-country, a 'flag of convenience' like the Cayman Islands, or Panama, or the Channel Islands, but on-shore. Enter Luxembourg.

Luxembourg's sovereignty is a freak of geo-politics. Historically it was a fortress on the Franco-German-Belgian border changing hands between the three, with intermittent periods of autonomy. Thanks to an "exception" in E. U. banking laws Luxembourg is now a post-modern city-state with a financial service monoculture: a bank with a flag,

Architecture, in Luxembourg City, with 70,000 inhabitants and 270 banks, is bank architecture. Banks saturated the historic city years ago; now a new *zone bancaire* of impressive dimensions spreads across the Kirchberg Plain, above the old city and just facing the European Parliament.

One hears no tales of buried treasure beneath the Kirchberg Plain. Here money is more godlike: omnipotent, omnipresent, and immaterial. Digitized wealth: financial "products," such as derivatives replace gold; Michael Leeson replaces *Goldfinger*.

Contemporary bank architecture attempts to reconcile the abstractness and invisibility of their real activities, with traditional images of wealth and probity. Such contradictory programs are, of necessity, problematic. The functional program dictates minimum structures that provide space, light and ventilation for the computers and their human servo-mechanisms; the public relations program dictates an imposing structure of precious materials. The second program prevails, but without credibility. The result is an architecture of humorless bad faith. The reigning spirit is not one of confidence but of the confidence-man, and if one thinks of the Kirchberg Plain as a kind of "Vegas Strip," with banks standing in for casinos the idea becomes clear: the differences are more apparent than real. The theme and variation of corporate *kitsch* is played by the "official" architects: Bohm, Meier, *et al.* with similar results. Architecture is irrelevant. It makes very little difference what these building look like so long as they give the same text:

"I AM A BANK, PRUDENT, YET PROGRESSIVE. TRUST ME."

This text originally appeared in *L'Architecture d'Aujourd'hui*, no. 300 (Sept. 1995).

A Better Tomorrow

Any discussion of housing should acknowledge the scores of million of persons globally without shelter or the reasonable hope of acquiring it, and the discussion would be incomplete without considering how homeless persons are addressed, or represented in the visual arts. Which is not to imply that art can offer a definitive view of the homeless. Contemporary cinema, for example, often reduces 'the homeless' to a kind of Hogarthian local color.

Homeless people have been around a long time, and in large enough numbers to constitute a culture, in the sense that one can speak of IBM or Microsoft as having a 'corporate culture.' Homelessness is its antithesis and its mirror, a 'discorporate' culture. Unlike the *nomenklatura*, the homeless are not yet a hereditary class in most parts of the First World. They are the downwardly mobile, evicted from a higher station in life.

In the less popular arts the homeless are often cited to provoke a critique of the larger, housed, society, interrogating the means of survival at the bottom and the social system that creates a permanent underclass *by choice*.

Anthony Hernandez's images of homeless sites, made in Southern California in the 1980s, can be read as an index of what one may have if one has nothing. From the mountains of trash discarded by the employed and housed the unemployed and unhoused find the minimum materials of survival: plastic bags and water bottles, shards of drywall and plywood, and of course, shopping carts. Extending the architectural metaphor one might say that if Hernandez discovered the native genius of anonymous, ephemeral, architecture, then Krzysztof Wodiczko could be considered the Buckminster Fuller of the dispossessed.

Wodiczko's initial homeless project *The Homeless Projection: A Proposal For Union Square* (1986) was made as a series of projected works intended to subvert the iconography of power in the public space. *The Homeless Vehicle Project* (1988-89), and its spin-off the *Poliscar* (1991) are more difficult to fix, targeting simultaneously several sore spots in the body politic. Perfectly feasible, the proposal is both monstrous – Swiftian – in the sense that it seems to accept the permanence of the homeless, and subversive insofar as it proposes a rolling critique-in-practice of the social order that deterritorialized them in the first place. *The Homeless Vehicle* is a machine designed to open the question of what is 'public' space.

Like a gypsy wagon it combines habitation and workplace: a hopper for the collection of recyclables, one of the few economic bases for people who are homeless. Santa Monica, California, one of America's richest cities, has both one of the highest per capita homeless populations and one (inadvertently) of the most effective recycling programs in the United States. As a result, the homeless become the engine of small-scale environmental clean-up, another 'Swiftian' implosion of two forms of political correctness.

The Homeless Vehicle, realized after extensive and scrupulously documented market research, is one of the most ingeniously over-designed products of the Eighties, a semiotic hybrid of hospital gurney, trashcan, space capsule and coffin, very consciously charged with the associations of each. Both practical and intensely disquieting it is a device that simultaneously ameliorates the misery of the dispossessed and reminds the haves that for millions of their fellow citizens the home of the future is no home at all.

To ensure domestic tranquility and provide for the common defense, the Nation of the Homeless would be granted limited autonomy in the regulation of its internal affairs. *i.e.* self-policing and in control of its channels of internal communication.

As the artist put it: "The name of the vehicle, the *Poliscar*, derives from the same root as police, policy, politics – namely the Greek word for the city-state, *polis*. In ancient Greece the word referred more to a state of society characterized by a sense of community and participation of the citizens (*polites*) than to an institution or place."

The *Poliscar* functions as a communications center, a watchdog, and as another spectral reminder of the visibility of people whom normal society would prefer to simply go away.

The point is, of course, that artists have been limited to just that degree of intervention: to represent, to make visible. At the basis of such intervention is the Benthamite ideal of the political discourse, according to which visibility, even transparency, is an inherent good. This idea might benefit from re-examination. In today's electronic panopticon visibility may bring only visibility, which is to say that artists are usually only able to engage a dialogue with persons already predisposed to have an interest in art and social issues. Those persons are usually neither the homeless nor the active conscious oppressors of the homeless.

Do homeless people benefit from publicity? Sometimes. Have artists sheltered, or fed, or even given meaningful visibility to anyone outside the art world? Rarely. Which is not to question the good faith of artists engaging social issues but to remark on the astonishing bad faith of a society that can valorize socially critical art while ignoring the issues that it raises.

This text originally appeared as "Sans-abri, sans lendemain," in *L'Architecture d'Aujourd'hui*, no. 303 (Sept. 1996).

The Painter of Modern Life

For the past thirty years the overwhelming majority of photographic works of major importance were produced by persons who did not consider themselves (and, if fortunate, were not considered by others) to be photographers. Artists as diverse as John Baldessari, Bernd and Hilla Becher, Christian Boltanski, Victor Burgin, Sophie Calle, Fischli/Weiss, Richard Prince, Ed Ruscha, Jeff Wall, *et. al.*, in very different and mutually opposing ways, defined a practice in opposition to, or simply in disregard of, photography's parochial history. Most of these artists began by using photographs as notations in works, which in a broad sense could be called conceptual. Jeff Wall's relation to photography was somewhat different. Following a brief and largely disavowed flirtation with pure Conceptualism in the late 1960s, Wall re-defined his objective to be the rehabilitation of "instructive representation" from the Baudrillardian abyss and, via technologies unavailable to his predecessors, such as large-scale color photography and computer-aided-production, its re-insertion into contemporary art, a goal that many of his colleagues regarded as anachronistic. *Picture for Women*, of 1978, was the second piece in his newly created style but the first to gain international attention. Charged with references to Manet, but speaking in a particularly modern idiom, *Picture for Women* was the foundation upon which Wall's practice would be built.

Wall's erudition and conceptual rigor offered an alternative to the anti-intellectualism that dominated the art market during the 1980s, and it was against that inhospitable background that

Wall achieved a number of his most distinctive works, the benchmarks against which his work, and that of many others, would be judged. Which might suggest why his long-awaited mid-career exhibition, seen here at the Jeu de Paume, and confined to works made between 1989 and 1994, was such a letdown. The specter haunting the Jeu de Paume was Wall himself.

Measured against his more selective output of the 80s it seems clear that in recent years Wall had not always attained the high standards he set for himself. But exhibitions serve the public good in many ways, and one of them might even be to disappoint. Artistic strategies, like other systems, yield more information about themselves at points of dysfunction than when they're running smoothly, and it could be more useful in understanding Wall's work to examine the "uneven" Jeff Wall of 1989-1994 rather than the seamless Jeff Wall of 1978-1989.

For few artists have the "politics of representation," and the "politics of presentation" been more crucially and consistently linked. Noting Conceptual Art's central contradiction, that the dematerialization of the art object in no way resulted in its decommodification, Wall dismissed the entire bogus question in favor of an overtly high-end presentation: large-scale cibachrome transparencies exhibited in self-illuminated boxes. His strategy served two ends, the first to distinguish Wall's work from other photography, and second, to give his works a visual autonomy technically impossible with large-scale color photographic prints.[1] With this technique Wall produced some of the most beautiful objects of the last twenty years.[2] Though hardly market-driven – perhaps, at the outset, its antithesis – Wall's presentation strategies found a positive resonance in a marketplace that regards beauty as a "quality", rather than a position in a dialectic battlefield, and the "masterpiece" a still-viable notion.[3]

What Wall retained from Conceptualism was its assertion of the primacy of language. Using the light-box as his proscenium, Wall staged a number of his best tableaux around situations depicting the conditions of speech: the physical and social spaces in which communication can flourish, such as *The Storyteller* or *The Diatribe*, or be refused (*No*), or internalized (*Picture for Women*), or suppressed (*Bad Goods* and *The Mimic*), or frozen (*The Outburst*, or *The Eviction)*....

In these works Wall never lost sight of the central question of who may speak, who may be a subject – who may be fully human...and who may not. The rage to speak and the rage to be heard forms the core around which many of Wall's most powerful works revolve. As with Peter Greenaway, rage energizes Wall's best work, and, as with Greenaway, the demands of rage often rescue his works from his own tendency to pedantry.

Another significant point of correspondence with Greenaway is that both charge their imagery with multiple levels of quotation and reference, a tactic that assures a resonance from art historians who are, after all, trained (one is almost tempted to say, *bred*) to seek just such correspondences. But as the art and architecture of the 1980s demonstrated, citation is not necessarily synonymous with thought; in some cases it may be its opposite. If citation can deepen and multiply the meanings embedded in a work, it can also become a ritualized game of seduction between the artist and his audience, each flattering the other's erudition. In Greenaway and in Wall one finds both.

In contrast to the generally lowered level of the late work,

Wall produced two of his most thoughtful and ambitious pieces in this same period. *Dead Troops Talk*, and *Restoration*, reference heroic battlefield painting of the 19th Century, and might even be considered as late entries in that genre. Both thematize the reconstruction of history. In *Dead Troops Talk* history is represented as nightmare: resurrection not from, but in death; a metaphor for our present perception of the once-feared Red Army. It is a work which might be compared, without embarrassment, to the late Goya that it emulates. In *Restoration*, Wall literally illustrates the construction and rehabilitation of meaning: the painting-over of history, in this case a piece of history that all the participants, except the Swiss, would prefer to forget: the surrender of the French Army to the Swiss after failing to relieve the Prussian siege of Belfort.[4]

And also, perhaps, a reference to another history: two women stand gazing outward from the image with a stance and countenance recalling Wall's *Young Workers* of 1978. Both works merit, and have received, individual monographs.[5]

One genre of Wall's work which remains unchanged is the bucolic landscape. Starting with *The Bridge* and *The Jewish Cemetery* of 1980, and continuing through *Coastal Motifs* of 1989 through *Park Drive* of 1994, these apparently unstaged, low-energy works are a parenthesis between Wall's other, more complex and, for better or worse, more histrionic efforts.

Most of Wall's other works from the early 1990s, by radically under or over-shooting their mark, unfortunately fail to generate the subtle tension that characterized the best of his earlier work. Many, like *Diagonal Composition, Some Beans, An Octopus, Adrian Walker, An Artist* never transcend the banality of their subject (Briony Fer's impressive apology notwithstanding)[6] while others,

A Ventriloquist at a Birthday Party in October 1947, *Vampire's Picnic*, *A Fight On the Sidewalk*, and the puerile *The Giant* – all the works in the "carnivalesque" genre – are so overwrought as to be drained of either conviction or authority. Among Wall's many incursions into painting's lesser genres, none has served him so poorly as his fascination with the grotesque. What is intended as a critical reworking of a kitsch genre becomes merely another instance of the same. Only by accepting at face value Wall's assertion that his practice aspires to the encyclopedic is it possible to imagine these works as the products of the same mind that produced the memorable earlier works.

If this seems harsh, it is only to say that Jeff Wall's intellect, though keen, is not, always, already, all-triumphant. That Wall is one of the most interesting artists working in the past 15 years is not in question, but whether all of his works are masterpieces is. In raising this question one must also acknowledge that to make any qualitative distinction between Wall's works is now, if not heretical, certainly futile; critical discourse, like the free market of goods inevitably gravitates toward monopoly, and most of the criticism surrounding Wall has entered its totalitarian phase: panegyric is the only acceptable rhetoric.[7] For an artist this is a seductive and dangerous position. It has been, in the recent past, the condition of artists such as Frank Stella, Cindy Sherman, and David Salle, a point that hardly requires elaboration.

[1] Large-scale color photographs are not so autonomous in exhibition as they seem in reproduction. Like glass curtain-wall buildings, their surface is discontinuous, a mass of multiple reflections which materialize and de-materialize the image in unpredictable ways depending upon ambient light.
[2] "I always try to make beautiful pictures." Jeff Wall, in an interview with Els Barents, *Transparencies* (Munich: Schirmer /Mosel, 1986).

[3] "...masterpieces are those works which deny the possibility, now, of masterpieces...Artists experience art as a process. Art historians experience art as a series of 'masterpieces'." Joseph Kosuth, "On Masterpieces," *Art After Philosophy and After. Collected Writings 1966-1990* (Cambridge: The MIT Press, 1991).
[4] The Bourbaki Panorama in Lucerne. *see below*
[5] Terry Atkinson, *Jeff Wall: Dead Troops Talk* (Lucerne: Kunstmuseum, 1993).
Arielle Pelenc, *Jeff Wall: Restoration* (Lucerne: Kunstmuseum, 1994).
[6] Briony Fer, *Jeff Wall* (Chicago: Chicago Museum of Contemporary Art, and Paris: Jeu de Paume, 1995).
[7] See Jean-Francois Chevrier, "Play, Drama, Enigma," in *Jeff Wall* (1995), *op. cit.* as an example of public relations cross-dressed as scholarship. Happily this is not a condition shared by Wall himself, whose prose and interviews are models of self-critical distance. See: "Three Excerpts From A Discussion With T. J. Clark, Claude Gintz, Serge Guilbaut, and Anne Wagner, " *Parkett #* 22, 1989, and/or "Traditions and Counter-Traditions In Vancouver Art: A Deeper Background For Ken Lum's Work," *Lectures* (Rotterdam: Witte de With, 1990).

Additional Bibliography

Ingrid Fischer Jonge, "The Repressed Encounter," *Jeff Wall* (Humlebaek, Denmark: Louisiana Museum of Modern Art, 1992).
Robert Lindsey and Verena Auffermann, *Jeff Wall: The Storyteller* (Frankfurt: Museum für Moderne Kunst, 1992).
Martin Schwandler, "Dead Troops Talk" (Luzern, Switzerland: Kunstmuseum Luzern, 1993).

This text originally appeared as "Jeff Wall, peintre de la vie moderne," in *L'Architecture d'Aujourd'hui*, no. 305 (June, 1996).

Fishes and Submarines

Wittgenstein: I think I'm going away again
Keynes: ...not the Soviet Union?
Wittgenstein: And what's wrong with the Soviet Union?
Keynes: The place is one enormous labor camp.
Wittgenstein: There's nothing wrong with labor.
Keynes: There is if they shoot you for not doing it.
Wittgenstein: ...I'm going to Ireland.
Keynes: In Ireland they shoot you if you *do* work.

Derek Jarman, *Wittgenstein* (1993)

The relation between mental and physical labor has been debated in the art world for the last 150 years, opposing "classless Bohemians" (art-for-art's sake) against the "art-workers" who prefer to stand shoulder to shoulder with their proletarian comrades: Baudelaire *vs.* Courbet; Duchamp *vs.* Tatlin and perhaps at the moment, Chris Burden *vs.* Allan Sekula.

Burden and Sekula are successful, mid-career, Euro-American male artists living in Los Angeles, and teaching at elite Southern California schools. Each participated in the well-known Los Angeles / Vienna axis of mutual fascination, Burden with a retrospective exhibition at the Museum of Applied Arts (MAK) and Sekula as a one of the centerpieces of the Styrian Autumn Festival in Graz. Other than sheer circumstance the only point of comparison between them is that each, in very different ways, foregrounds issues of industrial labor and heavy materials, proposing mutually exclusive artistic strategies of resistance in the face of a totalizing *fin-de-siècle* global capitalism. Sekula's practice is grounded in dialectical materialism, Burden's in a program of heroic transgressive action.

I. FISHES

Allan Sekula was and to some extent remains primarily known as a theoretician who also practices, rather than the other way around. His reputation accreted glacially over 25 years, largely through the influence of his writing and teaching, culminating in his present positions of influence on the editorial boards of *October*, and by extension, the M.I.T. Press, and his position at the California Institute of the Arts.

His first published writings interrogated and indicted the already moribund photographic art establishment's role in the invention of (specious) meaning and (undeserved) value in the commercial/cultural exchange of photographic imagery. Forceful in their moment – Sekula was among the first to challenge the hegemony of the old regime, his erstwhile adversaries (*e.g.* the Museum of Modern Art's Photography Department and George Eastman House) are now so completely discredited that many of these texts read like dispatches from a victorious but distant and half-forgotten war.[1]

Complementing his critical texts Sekula produced bodies of photographic works illustrating the kind of practice that he proposed to replace "Modernism," which by the mid-1970's had become a curse-word. These early works were problematic: however brilliantly Sekula trashed the dominant art practice he was initially unable to deliver more than the barest rudiments of a convincing alternative procedure, either in his own works (the too-mute *This Ain't China, 1974*, or its opposite, the overwrought *School Is A Factory*, 1982) or in the works of other art-workers that he championed. (Martha Rosler's *The Bowery In Two Inadequate Descriptive Systems*, or Fred Lonidier's *The Health and Safety Game: Fictions Based On Fact.*)

In his early texts the dispassionate, mocking voice of the dialectician usually eluded Sekula; his tone was more that of a Socialist Savanarola, brimming with high moral outrage which, however well founded, often ill-served his ends. (Capitalist propaganda succeeds where Socialist propaganda demonstrably fails, partly because the right takes persuasion seriously, while the left prefers to talk to itself.)

The most notable exception is *Aerospace Folktales* (1973) a quasi-sociological study of a laid-off Lockheed engineer, Sekula's father, a victim of one of the periodic troughs in the aerospace industry's boom-bust cycle. Sekula photographed the engineer's apartment, his family and their artifacts. Sekula interviewed the engineer, a proud member of the last generation of Americans who could reasonably believe that a college degree was a ticket to middle-class security. He interviewed the engineer's wife, whose undeniably working-class background gives her a far more realistic grasp of the family's social realities than her husband. Sekula appended his own commentary, a furious critique of his father's internalization of the dogmas of a system that has brought him to joblessness.

" ...my father never earned fifty thousand a year...my father never owned any stock...here he is living on unemployment and he sounds like the Lockheed chairman of the board...I mean he thinks this is all the dysfunction of a perfectly equitable system...."

Aerospace Folktales derives its power less from its implicit

Oedipal conflict or its status as a kind of proto-identity art (one should not accuse Sekula of that) than from the clarity and passion of direct experience. It was the first indication of what Sekula, when at his best, could achieve. Two decades later in *Fish Story* (1995) his voice rings with equal authority, but this time on a broader and more distant subject.

Marxism's strategic goal is immutable: the installation of a rational, just economic order, based in the communal ownership of the means of production by the proletariat. It follows that a dialectical materialist would be concerned with material itself, the stuff from which the industrial proletariat by dint of its labor creates surplus value. (It is exactly this allegiance to materiality that gives Lawrence Weiner's work its gravity.) And *materia*, and the physical exchange of the world's goods, is the armature upon which Allan Sekula built *Fish Story*.

"What one sees in a harbor is the concrete movement of goods. This movement can be explained in its totality only through recourse to abstraction. Marx tells us this, even if no one is listening anymore. If the stock market is the site in which the abstract character of money rules, the harbor is the site in which material goods appear in bulk, in the very flux of exchange...."

Fish Story tracks the physical movement of wealth, from hinterlands to the port to the open seas and back again. Wealth as raw material, as finished goods, as productive facilities, and, of course, as labor itself, the ugliest side of trans-oceanic traffic, bodies exporting themselves from less to a more survivable export platforms (and, sometimes, to the consternation of earlier immigrants, to the metropolitan countries themselves.)

Given a clear strategic objective, a good Marxist can shift tactics as needed, and in *Fish Story* Sekula appears to have done just that: to no longer let the devil have all the good tunes. Sekula's previous disdain for the seductive, spectacular qualities of the photographic image has been replaced with a tactic of co-opting these very qualities to fashion a parallel counter-text. Not that he has abandoned "constructive" in favor of "creative" photography but that he has reframed the latter inside the former; stereotypically beautiful color images functioning as citations of "esthetic" photography, contextually charged with a self-reflexive critical distance. (Calling into question Benjamin Buchloch's rather disingenuous assertion that Sekula's work is culturally illegible by the codes of late (or post-) Modernist photographic practice.)[2] He also polished his rhetorical skills: before he declaimed, now he insinuates. A cognitive space seems to open for the reader to participate in the construction of meaning.

To cite only one of many of Sekula's instructive tales of seafaring life, he traces the optic of maritime representation from the panoramic 17th century Dutch ships-in harbor painting through the monocular vision of the submarine periscope, to the microscopic close-up of the maggot-infested meat that triggers the *Potemkin* mutiny; the utopic vision of the freedom of the seas framing the dystopic authoritarianism of shipboard life – from which issues the "threat or hope" of mutiny. On his geopolitical map of the high seas Sekula charts the history of industrial capitalism – and its socialist nemesis. The wine-dark sea has always been a privileged site for projects of epic ambition, and if one accepts the definition of a masterpiece as a work in which an artist's full arsenal of resources are marshaled as never before to bring coherence to an unruly and epic theme, *Fish Story* is Sekula's masterpiece.

Fish Story debuted at the Witte de With, in Rotterdam. On the day of my visit the only other persons in the exhibition were a Parisian gallerist and a Dutch independent curator. Chris Dercon, the organizer of the show and book, observed that, "this is an exhibition for specialists," and unhappily he was probably correct. The workers Sekula speaks about, and in a sense for, were nowhere to be seen, as if to illustrate the difficulties confronting an artist who wishes his work to be both intelligent and intelligible to a wider public. Discursive artworks can easily find a resonance in the museums, the academy, and the art media, but are insulated from a broader public whose many, and conflicting, received notions of what art is rarely include the possibility that it is an arena of socially critical inquiry.

Nevertheless, for those willing to make the effort Sekula reminds us that as we gape at the virtual heavens (whose constellations are charted on the business pages of all of our leading newspapers, perhaps near where the ship movements used to be) our feet are still planted in the mud; that most of the world's product is heavy and bulky and must be transported over vast distances by the slowest and cheapest means, which whenever possible is by water; and that the labor of making and moving most of the world's goods, though now banished to the margins of the capitalist "home office" countries, remains strenuous, dangerous, dirty, and underpaid. Wherever the infobahn promises to deliver us there remains important unfinished business between consumers and producers of the world's goods.

II. SUBMARINES

Chris Burden's work doesn't privilege the sea and his encounters with blue water have largely been in human-powered craft or in small-scale models. His claim to epic proportion lies elsewhere in the realm of heroic self-invention. Chris Burden has always, or nearly always, been famous; the notoriety following his second performance, *Shoot*, assured that. In November, 1971, Burden had himself shot in the arm by a marksman/friend with a 22-long rifle fired from a distance of 5 meters. "In this instant I was sculpture." *Shoot* launched a mythology that transcended the art world. When *Esquire* magazine published "Three Faces For the Seventies," Burden's was among them, alongside porno star Linda Lovelace and F.B.I. Director L. Patrick Grey. While Sekula was concerned with interrogating the mechanisms of art-world valorization, Burden was engaged in hijacking them, in a kind of critique-in-practice. His interest in mediatized celebrity pinnacled in a work he made in 1976, a 30 second spot broadcast on two New York TV stations, listing names of the best-known artists in history – plus his own: "Leonardo de Vinci, Michelangelo, Rembrandt, Vincent Van Gogh, Pablo Picasso, Chris Burden" and closing with the disclaimer: "paid for by Chris Burden – artist."

Between 1971 and 1974 Burden made thirty performances, nearly all involving himself in danger, pain, or risk. He was imprisoned in a school locker for five days (his Master's Thesis project), shot, electrocuted, kicked down a flight of stairs at the Basel Art Fair, and crucified (to a Volkswagen beetle). He was filmed crawling nearly naked through a field of broken glass. (The film was later broadcast on L.A. T.V.) Sometimes his risks were legal: faking a hit-and-run accident in front of a Los Angeles art gallery with himself as the blanket-shrouded victim; holding an interviewer at knife-point in a local, live TV broadcast; shooting at a 747 departing from LAX. (Some said that the bullets were blanks, but only Burden knows for sure.)

Burden was one among several artists exploring the use of the body as sculptural material, in a literalist response to the disappearance of the human figure from contemporary art. Bruce Nauman and Burden's former professor, Mowry Baden exhibited together in "Body Movements," at the La Jolla Museum of Art (now the Museum of Contemporary Art, San Diego) in early 1970. Burden's works were complimented by those of Vito Acconci, Bruce Nauman, Dennis Oppenheim, and Gina Pane, among others. For Nauman and Oppenheim body works were aspects of a broader investigation of sculptural possibilities. For Acconci and Burden, it was their only realized work, and with the exception of Acconci's *Seedbed* (1971), Burden's was the more transgressive. In the popular mind Burden's theater of cruelty was as much linked with terrorism as with sculpture. (Terrorism had a much better profile then.)

Acconci, Nauman, Oppenheim, and Pane tended to be the objects of their investigations whereas Burden was first and foremost the subject. Both *übermensch* and victim (but *übermensch* nevertheless, by virtue of his ability to endure what his audience would find unendurable), Chris Burden became CHRIS BURDEN, sculptural material and art-world personage par excellence, even if the art world was unsure of where to place him. In retrospect his position seems clearer, as a nexus between the use of the body as material and the body as the site of autobiographical inscription, an idea brought into the present in the work of artists like Matthew Barney and Sophie Calle.

Starting in 1975 with the B-Car, an energy-efficient soap-box-derby racer of Burden's own design and manufacture, Burden's interest began to encompass other forms of matter than his own body, particularly machinery, and the heavier the better. If Sekula's materialism is dialectical, and his household gods Marx, Engels, and Benjamin, Burden's relation to material is idealist: heavy, obdurate, threatening, matter bending through sheer heroic effort to artist's will, Burden might well number de Sade, Nietzsche, and (to the extent of his absorption with the etiology of power) Foucault among his mentors. Burden's ideology is elusive, and his work hardly "theory-driven," juxtaposing a boyish sense of wonder at the vastness of the physical universe and the power of its laws (*Scale Model of the Solar System*, *Speed of Light Machine* and *Frictionless Sled*, all from 1983; *Fist of Light*, 1992-93) with a critique of our application of those laws and our powerlessness in the face of our creations (*Medusa's Head*, 1990, and its satellites *Medusa's Flying Moon*, and the *Five Moonettes*, 1994). *Medusa's Head* is an irregular sphere, weighing several tons and measuring four meters in diameter suspended from the ceiling, whose scarred surface is of a dead world choked in the stranglehold of industrial technology, represented by intertwined networks of toy train tracks. It is one of the most unpleasant objects created since Surrealism, a perfect emblem of Burden's "love-hate" relationship between man and machine, a world deformed and imprisoned by the technologies Burden often represents as toys.

Boy toys: a male world, made of stereotypically butch stuff: cars and trucks and trains and planes and ships; weapons and the machinery of past and future wars; heavy construction and heavier demolition. For as surely as there is Feminist art there is also Mannist art, an art that privileges the viewpoint of half of the human race and excludes – at least as subject – the other half, and while Burden's art neither oppresses nor demeans women, it also doesn't pay a lot of attention to *their* stereotypical concerns.

Burden's ambiguity is evident in *The Big Wheel* (1979), a ludicrously simple device exhibited at the Centre Pompidou in 1994. "...3-ton cast iron flywheel [244 cm in diameter] mounted in a vertical position and set in motion by the rear tire of a motorcycle. The iron wheel was accelerated to a speed of 220 revolutions per minute. *The Big Wheel* would spin freely for 2 1/2 hours...."

The Big Wheel (American slang for someone powerful) is a clear metaphor of the dichotomies of man and machine, hero and victim: a (relatively) little man, with his (again, relatively) little motor, setting forces in motion that he is powerless to control or to stop. Or, viewed from the other side of the mirror, the parable of the Juggernaut is inverted: the Chaplinesque little guy, with ingenuity and some daring, becomes Prometheus, and moves a mountain.

Beginning in 1979 with *Atomic Alphabet*, *Pearl Harbor*, and *The Reason For the Neutron Bomb*, Burden turned more of his attentions to mechanized warfare and weapons of mass destruction – about a fifth of his output since then. (What seems strange isn't Burden's preoccupation with the destructive forces of war, but the absence of this issue in the work of most other artists of his generation, for whom Atomic War was literally a household word.)

Burden is not usually grouped with "political" artists, yet there were strong elements of social critique in Burden's work. Sekula interrogated the legitimacy of the museum structure in the creation of value in several closely reasoned critical texts; Burden literally exposed the museum's feet of clay (*Exposing the Foundation of the Museum*, 1986-1988). His fascination with war toys not withstanding, Burden is not a closet – nor any other kind of – militarist. His unambiguous comment on the reality, as opposed to the spectacle, of war was *The Other Vietnam Memorial* (1991), a list of "...three million Vietnamese names, symbolizing the North and South Vietnamese killed during the U.S. involvement from 1968-1973, in the Vietnamese Civil War...." A terse reminder to clarify who were the victims and who were the aggressors, and a pointed antidote to the official memorial in Washington, D.C., which shamefully conflates honest mourning for the dead with a bogus image of national victimization.

Allan Sekula would very likely take exception to Burden's vision of work, and workers, though his sailors and stevedores might find much to like in the image of the working-class hero. But, in the end, people who work hard for their living have a sharp nose for condescension, intentional or not, and to someone who digs ditches all day, *every day*, the spectacle of Chris Burden as a Sunday Stakhanovite might seem as effete as the rustified picnics of Marie Antoinette did to the real (and hungry) peasants whose costumes the courtiers, in a grotesque parody of egalitarianism, appropriated. Ultimately, the lives of the "other" are equally inaccessible to Sekula as they are to Burden, and their claims to our attention rest less on the degree of identity that they share with their subjects than on the idea that the view from outside also has its value.

Sekula's program offers a disciplined, vital counterforce to the ideology of runaway capitalism and a welcome, if not entirely logical, inversion of the official wisdom that "communism failed *ergo* capitalism must work." Burden's project includes the ongoing battle against authority, irrespective of its ideological guise. Their positions, which are mutually exclusive, have placed them, in certain instances, the same side of the barricades. And, ironically, as major players in the system that they love to hate.

[1] Editor's note: Many of Sekula's texts were collected in Allan Sekula, *Photography Against the Grain: essays and photoworks, 1973-1983* (Halifax: Press of the Nova Scotia College of Art and Design, 1984).
[2] See Benjamin H.D. Buchloh, "Allan Sekula: Photography between Discourse and Document," *Fish Story* (Rotterdam: Witte de With, 1995).

This text originally appeared as "Burden & Sekula, poissons et sous-marins," in *L'Architecture d'Aujourd'hui*, no. 312 (September 1997).

Untitled: Felix Gonzales-Torres

"All the new thinking is about loss. In this it resembles all the old thinking."

Robert Haas, "Meditations at Lagunitas," *Praise*[1]

In "Rosencrantz and Guildenstern Redux: The Artist's Voice after the Death of the Author," David Hickey quoted a colleague of artist Ray Johnson, upon learning of Johnson's suicide: "A smart career move."[2] Hickey explained his cynical and unoriginal remark (it was earlier attributed to Gore Vidal about Truman Capote's death) with the argument that death, and only death, provides the necessary closure for an objective assessment of the artist's contribution. Hickey is probably correct in the long term, but the short term is more problematic. When an artist dies prematurely his work is often only viewed through the prism of a truncated mortality: criticism collapses into anecdote or, worse, hagiography. For artists like Diane Arbus or Robert Mapplethorpe, death confers both a questionable martyrdom and an irrefutable proof of authenticity: "They were not tourists in the world that they moved through; they shared the ultimate complicity with their subjects. They died as they lived; they died for their art." And so forth.

For Felix Gonzales-Torres, whose work thematized the ephemerality and fragility of life, an early death compounds the risk that an unwanted sentimentality might infect the elegiac with the mawkish, which is contrary to what his art demanded. Gonzales-Torres was many things: Cuban immigrant; gay man; post-studio artist, mourning lover, a person with AIDS, and an articulate and sympathetic spokesman for all of these facets of his identity. He also possessed the finest artistic intelligence to emerge in American art in the last decade. His work has been displayed in solo exhibitions in America's most influential museums. His positions on art and social activism, delivered in conferences, lectures, and interviews transformed opposition art discourse. There was nothing in his art, his social engagement, or his statements that suggests that he perceived himself as a victim. His death last January left a relatively small but highly influential body of works in a variety of mediums and a deep lacuna in the landscape of contemporary American art.

The artistic milieu that Gonzales-Torres entered – New York in the late 80's – was a drastically impoverished one for a thoughtful artist. The waves of innovation that had swept the New York art world since 1945 had subsided, leaving behind a monolithic commercial edifice purpose-built for marketing reactionary to a newly created of class of speculators who demanded, and of course received, a traditional and easily comprehensible art. Oppositional practice mirrored (and perversely supported) the sterility of the market. Feminist artistic discourse devolved from the complexities of Eva Hesse into the simplistic sloganeering of Barbara Kruger. Gay art, in previous decades defined by artists such as Johns, Rauschenberg, and Warhol, was now characterized by a dominant practice of homoerotic pinups.

Gonzalez-Torres refused this (and every other) gay stereotype as repressive and, moreover, as playing directly into the hands of the homophobic ultra-right. Instead he adopted a strategy of *détournement*, subverting received forms of high culture-Minimalism, Conceptualism, *et. al.* to his own purposes. Appropriating the idiom of the master narrative, Gonzalez-Torres proposed an art with multiple and often conflicting readings. He mainstreamed the 'gay agenda' or *his* gay agenda, by addressing both gay and straight audiences with works that were not only personally and politically charged, but were a meditation on the conditions and possibilities of art. The themes of time (as instrument and arbiter of mortality) and of generosity (as an engine to defeat, or forestall mortality) are pervasive in Gonzalez-Torres' work. His allusions to mortality are sometimes blandly literal, as in *"Untitled" (Perfect Lovers),* 1987-1990, two synchronous battery-powered wall clocks placed side by side, marking the passage of time until one or the other falls out of sync, slows, and stops. His portraits invert the received notion of portraiture, 'immortalizing the sitter.' Timelines, installed as friezes, melding significant moments in his subject's lives with dates of contemporary historical events, imbedding them in the passage of time and the corruption of the flesh, an homage of sorts to the best-known unexecuted portrait of the last century, Dorian Gray.

In a much-published interview, Tim Rollins asked Gonzalez-Torres what he would like from his students.[3] He replied that he would like them to be generous. It was a revealing answer from an artist who placed such a high priority on generosity in his own work. The celebrated paper stacks and the arrangements of candy described by the artist as having an ideal height or weight and from which the visitor was invited to take one (or more) elements to be replaced as necessary from an endless supply, function as symbolic generosity wile alluding to another, impossible generosity: the hope of endless renewal, a secular realization of divine grace. This is the language of prayers and a gesture approaching transubstantiation, but like the wily priest, Gonzalez-Torres' gifts create obligations. The 'gift' work seems to fulfill an unkept promise of the 1960s, the decommodification of art, but they are not precisely that. Gonzalez-Torres proposes a transaction as old as the ritual of gift-giving: to accept an element of his work is to be implicated in its realization, and in its future.

In 1992 Gonzalez-Torres started his most eloquent works, twenty-four light sculptures consisting of twenty-four or forty-two, fifteen or twenty-five watt white light bulbs, distributed evenly over several meters of electrical cord. The works are identical, varying only in their titles and their installations, which is left to the discretion of the installed. Sublimely beautiful, yet so commonplace that outside the museum or gallery context they resist identification as art, the light strings are Gonzalez-Torres' ultimate gesture of implicating the perceiver in the construction of meaning.

"I didn't know how those pieces are best displayed. I don't have all the answers – you decide how you want it done. Whatever you want to do, try it. This is not some minimalist artwork that has to be exactly two inches to the left and six inches down. Play with it, please. Have fun. Give yourself that freedom. Put my creativity into question, minimize the preciousness of the piece...."

In 1995 the Guggenheim Museum organized a retrospective exhibition of Gonzalez Torres's works, which was exhibited at the Musée d'Art Moderne in Paris from April through June the following year. The installation of the Gonzales-Torres retrospective was uncommonly affecting. Exhibitions in L'ARC are most often installed to exploit the building's signature quality, its unbroken circular flow of space. Gonzalez-Torres exhibition ended abruptly in a cul-de-sac at the point where one would usually continue into the connecting galleries. This decision recalled Dani Karavan's *Homage to Walter Benjamin* at Portbou, Spain, where the visitor descends a steep staircase incised into a cliff facing the sea (*Somewhere Better Than This Place*) only to find his progress blocked by a wall of glass. Like Benjamin, he must retrace his steps, up the stairs and back to the world (*Nowhere Better Than This Place*).

[1] Robert Haas, *Praise* (New York: Ecco Press, 1979).
[2] Dave Hickey, "Rosencrantz and Guildenstern Redux: The Artist's Voice after the Death of the Author," *Between Artists: Twelve contemporary American artists interview twelve contemporary American artists*, ed. Lucinda Barnes (New York: A.R.T. Press, 1995) xi.
[3] "Felix Gonzalez-Torres, interviewed by Tim Rollins, 1993," in *Between Artists: Twelve contemporary American artists interview twelve contemporary American artists*, ed. Lucinda Barnes (New York: A.R.T. Press, 1995) 83-101.

This text originally appeared as "Felix Gonzales-Torres, (sans titre)," in *L'Architecture d'Aujourd'hui*, no. 306 (September 1996).

Auf diese Dinge gibt es keine Antwort

Last night I read a story from Simon Schama's *Landscape and Memory* that, in vastly reduced terms, I'd like to retell.[1] The beginning is worthy of an *Indiana Jones* adventure. The story begins in Italy, in the autumn of 1943. The country is divided between advancing allied armies in the south and the Germans, who, after the fall of Mussolini are determined to hold the center and north of the country for the Reich. A squad of Fascist militia, led by an elite corps of German SS officers has ransacked the Palazzo Balleani at Fontedamo, destroying whatever remained in the 18th century villa. Their mission was not to punish Balleani for his anti-Fascist sympathies, but to find a singular treasure, a 15th century Codex, of Tacitus' *Germania*, what Schama calls, without irony, "...the birth certificate of the German race."

Written in 98 A.D. it is the first known reference to Germany and to the Germans, as a people, and its value as National Socialist propaganda cannot be overestimated. Reichsmarshall Himmler himself ordered the repatriation of the Codex to Germany, where a new, "definitive" edition had been recently published – with Himmler's foreword. Its purpose was, of course, to remind the embattled Germans of their lineage: noble, warlike, and racially pure. Himmler was not the first to exploit Tacitus' text: *Germania* had been a touchstone of German nationalism for five centuries.

Disgusted with the decadence of Imperial Rome, Tacitus had portrayed the early Germans as nature's noblemen. Though

Barbarians, they were brave and warlike, monogamous, egalitarian, and – a part that certainly appealed to the Nazis – uncontaminated by intermarriage with other peoples. In short, everything that the Romans of the 1st Century were not.

More to the point of this discussion, Tacitus located his Germans in a landscape. They did not live in cities, but in clearings in the untracked German forest. The forest was the source of their sustenance, their ally in battle, and the place to where their remains were returned at death. Their gods dwelt in the forest, and their temples were the sacred groves of oak.

Throughout its history Germany has been represented by idealizations of the primeval forest. Schama cites Albrecht Altdorfer's *St. George and the Dragon*, 1510, as an early example, a line that he continues through Caspar David Friedrich, Anselm Kiefer to Joseph Beuys reforresting a German city with 7,000 oak trees as his contribution to Documenta VII.

The cathedral at Reims is the most ancient sacred site in France. It was on this site in 498 A.D. that Clovis converted to Christianity and by so doing formed the basis for what has become the modern French nation. French monarchs were crowned here and even today each President of the Republic has found occasion early in his administration to be photographed here. It is the symbol of the mixing of religious and civic authority, a mixture that 200 years after the French Revolution has not quite been untangled. It is also a symbol of the subjugation of French cultural identity to Rome, and with Classical history. The baptism of Clovis placed France within the sphere of the Mediterranean, rather than Nordic world-view, binding France, through Rome, to the ideals of Classical Greece.

After that France would never again be a forest, but a garden, an ordered Arcadian universe whose measure was man. Even its contradictions are subsumed into a harmonious whole. At least that's the perception. Reims doesn't look particularly whole, nor harmonious. As the last city between Paris and the advancing German armies of The Great War, Reims was pummeled by gun fire for years – and if in the nuclear age we forget how much damage simple artillery can wreak, a few minutes of CNN footage of Sarajevo can correct that misapprehension. Reims was rebuilt through the philanthropy of American robber barons: the Cathedral now faces Place Rockefeller, not far from the Carnegie Library. The Americans also donated their ideas of urban organization, reconstructing the concentric middle-age street plan with a grid system. Reims, now, doesn't look like much of anything at all, other than the prosperous, ethnically and architecturally diverse provincial capital that it is. But that's not so important to the Reimois. Nor to the French sense of identity: *La France*, *La belle France*, is a concept, so ideally perfect that it needs no vulgar concrete manifestation. No wilderness myths darken the French mind. "Pure" landscape rarely enters French art – just ask the Impressionists. When the landscape is represented it's classical, analytical, rational, and, of course instructive – just ask Poussin.

The point of these two stories isn't to meditate upon the imponderable differences between the French and German soul, but to illustrate that the concept of landscape itself already acknowledges that the land exists in the condition of a cognitive representation: the transformation of *pay* to *paysage*, or *Land* to *Landschaft*, is a meaning constructed out of and embedded in the requirements of an historical narrative, a meta-code that we then use to explain ourselves to ourselves and to others.

To imagine an *Absolute Landscape* would be to imagine a master narrative, one, which commanded the allegiance of all its listeners, an idea attractive, in a sense, for its sheer perversity.

[1] Simon Schama, *Landscape and Memory* (New York: Alfred A. Knopf, 1995).

This text originally appeared in *Absolute Landscape: Contemporary photography between illusion & reality* (Yokohama: Yokohama Museum of Art, 1997).

What does Possession Mean to You?

In four decades two films have become five. *Le Retour de Martin Guerre* (1982, dir. Daniel Vigne), gave birth to *Sommersby* (1993, dir. Jon Amiel) and *The Invasion of the Body Snatchers* (1956, dir. Don Siegel), followed by remake I (*The Invasion of the Body Snatchers*, 1978, dir. Philip Kaufman) and II (*Body Snatchers*, 1993, dir. Abel Ferrara). These five films are in fact one film, in so far as they all harp on the same question: identity theft.

The appeal of Martin Guerre's story comes in great measure from the notion that we can assign a specific moment to paradigmatic shifts in human consciousness, such as Petrarch's ascent of Mount Ventoux, and his subsequent annexation of landscape into the realm of esthetics. Martin Guerre's story is the first recorded and examined instance of what is now a most commonplace human condition, the crisis of identity, the idea that identity is not intrinsic but invented and contingent.

The story, in brief, is this: In 1556 a vagabond soldier returns from the wars to his native village of Artigat in the foothills of the Pyrennes. He had fled the village in disgrace 15 years earlier, leaving his inheritance, his young wife and their infant child. The returning man's features were familiar enough and he could recount at length and in intimate detail particulars of family and village life that could be known only to the missing man. The man's wife takes him in and they live together contentedly for two years, until a financial dispute within the family provokes an uncle to challenge the newcomer's identity. The wife, too, begins to suspect that the kind and wise man with whom she has shared her marriage bed is not the churlish Martin Guerre to whom she had been wed as a child, and that to ignore her suspicions is to court mortal sin. A legal process is launched to test the claims of the conflicting parties, and dozens of witnesses are called to testify for or against the authenticity of the man who calls himself Martin Guerre. The results of the first inquiry are inconclusive and a second proceeding is launched in nearby Toulouse. At the precise moment when the judges are about to hand down their decision in favor of the man (Arnaud du Tilh), the true Martin Guerre appears in the courtroom claiming by birthright his wife and property. Unmasked, the imposter confesses, begs the forgiveness of God and the woman he has dishonored, and is sentenced to death.

The story might have died with its principal actors had not de Coras thought it sufficiently extraordinary to record and publish the particulars of the case.[1] Since Coras' original account in 1561, the story of Martin Guerre has been retold in dozens of written works, the most recent and authoritative being Natalie Zemon Davis' *The Return of Martin Guerre*, in 1983, upon which the Daniel Vigne film of the same name was based.[2]

From de Coras' text we learn the criteria for establishing identity. In the 16th century, photographs, dental records, fingerprints, DNA tracing, and uniform record keeping are undreamed of, while widespread literacy lay hundreds of years in the future. Resemblance plays an important role, as is evident, but the predispositions of that period lent a further dimension to verisimilitude: persons with similar physiognomies were believed to have similar characters. Memory, too, is in the dock: the authenticity, or plausibility, of your memories of others (Arnaud du Tilh was said to have a prodigious memory), and their perceptions of you. And, most important, whether one could state one's case convincingly. These were the components of the definitive test of identity which was, you are the person others believe you to be. What has become today a social fact has its roots in another epoch's concept of legal fact. What was a legal curiosity in one period has become a general condition in another: the question of what is identity, how one can possess an identity and to what extent is that identity negotiable or alienable. It is little wonder why the story has grown in popularity over the years.

Even in the story that carries his name, Martin Geurre's identity remains shadowy. His presence, like that of the outer planets, is known through its influence on the other figures in this constellation: his wife, Bertrande de Rols; his impersonator, Arnaud du Tilh; and his judge, the scholarly Jean de Coras. The pitiable Martin Guerre is not the subject of his own history, which focuses on the prodigious audacity of his imposter. Guerre's identity is forever mingled with and eclipsed by that of the cleverer du Tilh, who through a bold appropriation, possessed two identities, his own and Guerre's.

The Invasion of the Body Snatchers was an instant cult classic when it first appeared in 1956. The body snatchers – we see them only as embryos, green pods resembling elongated watermelons, and then in their purloined bodies – seem to want only their victims' souls. The Body Snatchers left their victims material lives intact: "You get to keep your clothes, your apartment, your car…everything," a "snatched" friend explains to a reluctant Donald Sutherland in the 1978 remake. Though their project is to conquer the world and enslave the human race, their methods, like their victims, are eerily bland. We see them mete out no punishments to their captives; only exploitation of their victim's labor to help propagate the new species, reducing yuppies to longshoremen who load trucks and ships with green pods, destined for new zones of conquests. The victims seem zombie-like, dispirited, though not much more so than anyone else unaccustomed to stupefying labor would be in the course of such a task. "Body Snatchers" is a misnomer: they only wanted your soul.

America was very uneasy about the possession of its soul in those days. With over half of the world's economic power and near monopoly of its weapons of mass destruction, Americans nevertheless felt a profound insecurity for which *The Body Snatchers* were an ideal metaphor. The beauty of viewing *Body Snatchers* through the prism of Cold War politics was that it could be read from either right or left. Ultra-nationalists, exemplified by Joseph McCarthy, were crusading against a ubiquitous Red Menace which they believed had already infiltrated the government, the Army, the schools, the motion picture industry, the intelligentsia; even the drinking water was suspect. One could become infected without willing or knowing it, subliminally, as in one's sleep. You might retire one night a true American and wake up the next morning as a brainwashed cell in the Red Hordes. *Body Snatchers.*

The left, that is, the liberals, though far less vocal or powerful, had an opposing reason to fear for America's collective soul: the numbing conformity of the 1950s, in part the birth pains of the postwar consumer world and in part a reaction to widespread paranoia of the McCarthy period. The old American values of rugged individualism, independent thought, love of freedom, had been transformed into an unquestioning orthodoxy.

Body Snatchers is all too available to direct political readings, but the 1950s also gave birth to the most psychologically complicated cinematic work to ever deal with the question of created identity. *Vertigo* (1958, dir. Alfred Hitchcock) was "a film about a man in love with a dead woman," its author understated. Yet despite this tantalizing hint of necrophilia, one might say that it was a film about a man who undresses, and then dresses, a woman.

But the issue of possession, if not its Hollywood representation, long preceded, and long survived the simplicities of McCathryism. It touched a deeper question, put succinctly by Lewis Carroll's hashish smoking caterpillar "Who are *you*?"

Identity has been up for grabs for a long time. More and more. The most eloquent instance of the question of mistaken identity was posed by Hitchcock in *Vertigo*, perhaps the most written about and therefore most unviewable film since *Citizen Kane* (1941, dir. Orson Welles). *Vertigo*'s confounding of identity captured more of us – scholars and artists – than did the tale of Martin Guerre.

[1] Jean de Coras, *Arrest Memorable* (Lyon: Antoine Vincent, 1565).
[2] Natalie Zemon Davis, *The Return of Martin Guerre* (Cambridge: Harvard University Press, 1984).

What does Possession Mean to You? is the title of a seminal work by Victor Burgin from 1974.
This text was previously unpublished, composed ca. 1997.

Maybe it's About Kim Novak

Vertigo seems to me Hitchcock's masterpiece to date, and one of the four or five most profound and beautiful films the cinema has yet given us.

Robin Wood[1]

Wood's observation, made in the 1960s, sums up the present critical attitude toward *Vertigo*'s place in the history of cinema, though at the time of its release, and for many years afterward, it would have been difficult to find many English-speaking critics who would make such a claim for a film that was then seen as a confused and confusing box-office failure.

In the intervening years *Vertigo* has become one of the canonical texts of post-modern cinema and the unlocking of the secrets it encoded has become a cottage industry.

Vertigo's, and Hitchcock's, critical rehabilitation during the forty years since its release merits and has received its own separate study. But more than the passage of time that elevated *Vertigo* to its present iconic status, not the forty years but *those* forty years, and the emergence of new paradigms in critical studies. The devices that made *Vertigo* hard to grasp in its own time – its ellipses, disjunctions, floating identities, "destruction of trust with the viewer," and most of all its obsession with mirroring – have made it an inexhaustibly rich site of critical and artistic discourse in ours. One is reminded of Borges' Chinese scholar in "The Garden of Forking Paths." Asked what he is doing, he gives a seemingly contradictory reply: "I am writing a novel / I am building a labyrinth." Always / already post-modern, *Vertigo* seduces the critical viewer into its maze.

When Alfred Hitchcock came to Hollywood he knew that in the studio system no director, however free or powerful, was allowed to determine the final editing of his own films. Rather than foment a losing argument, Hitchcock rehearsed his actors for days, filmed them in one take, delivering what was, in effect, pre-edited footage to his studio bosses. The master of suspense hated being on the receiving end.

By the 1950s when Hitchcock had become accustomed to the adulation of his more serious, *i.e.* less commercial, colleagues at the *Cahiers du Cinema*, he devoted an increasing amount of his attentions to their good opinions as well as to his American box office. This period gave us *Vertigo*; the most nihilistic film ever released by a major Hollywood studio. It pleased Hitchcock to describe *Vertigo* as "a film about a man in love with a dead woman," but its perversity ranged far wider than its specious whiff of necrophilia. A large part of our present fascination with *Vertigo* is Hitchcock's uncanny anticipation of a critical discourse unborn and unimagined in the 1950s, as though a director whose attention extended to the smallest details, could somehow also manipulate – from beyond the grave – the critical reading of his *oeuvre* by artists and theorists of the 80s and 90s, with the same facility that he manipulated movie-goers during his lifetime, laying snares to be sprung decades later, a Hitchcockian doomsday machine.

Vertigo *seems at first to be about a man's impotence in the face of, or faced with the task of sustaining his desire; perhaps, on second thought, about the precariousness of human verticality altogether. But it turns out to be about the specific power of a man's fantasy to cause him to not merely forego reality – that consequence is as widespread as the sea – but to gear every instant of his energy toward a private alteration of reality…*Vertigo *is just a movie, but no other movie I know* *so purely conveys the sealing a mind within a scorching fantasy. James Stewart is not so much of an anti-hero, but the totality of his longing- and the terrorizing defacement of his object's identity which his longing comes to require mimics that convolution of consciousness which transcends idolatry in favor of the fantastic reality of God, that point past imagination in which happiness and truth coalesce.*[2]

It's said that *Vertigo* is a film about a man who undresses and dresses a woman, with a passion so absolute as to be confused with love, or with love's desire, and inherent in that is the question of a medium in which dressing and undressing can have the same significance.

(And what sort of medium might this be?)[3]

A medium in which an off-screen dispute between the director and his heroine can be replayed in front of the camera.

No, I won't do *it…I don't* like *it.*

With the exception of Victor Burgin, very few people have been more deeply engaged with *Vertigo* than Chris Marker.

He wrote me that only one film had been possible of capturing impossible memory, insane memory: Alfred Hitchcock's Vertigo. In the spiral of the titles he saw time covering a field ever wider as it moved away…a cyclone whose present moment contains forever motionless the eye. In San Francisco he had made a pilgrimage to all of the film's locations. The florist, Podesta Baldochi, where James Stewart spies on Kim Novak, he the hunter, she the hunted – or was it the other way around? The tiles hadn't changed. He had driven up and down the hills of San Francisco where Jimmie Stewart as" Scottie" follows Kim Novak, "Madeleine." It seems to be a question of trailing, of enigma, of murder, but in truth its a question of power and freedom, of melancholy and dazzlement, so carefully coded in the spiral that you could miss it, and not discover immediately that this vertical space in reali-

ty stands for the vertigo in time. He had followed all the trails, even to the cemetery of Mission Dolores where Madeleine had gone to pray at the grave of a woman, long since dead, whom she could not have known. He followed Madeleine, as Scottie had done, to the Museum of the Legion of Honor, before the portrait of a dead woman she should not have known, and on the portrait, as in Madeleine's hair, the spiral of time. The small Victorian hotel where Madeleine had disappeared, disappeared itself. Concrete had replaced it at the corner of Eddy and Gough. On the other hand, the sequoia was still in Muir Woods. On it Madeleine traced the short distance between two of those concentric lines that measure the age of the tree and said, "Here I was born and here I died." He remembered another film in which the passage was quoted. The sequoia was the one in the Jardin des Plantes in Paris and the hand pointed to a place outside the tree, outside of time. The painted horse at San Juan Bautista, his eye that looked liked Madeleine's. Hitchcock invented nothing. It was all there. He had run under the arches of the promenade in the mission as Madeleine had run to her death, or was it hers? from this fake tower, the only thing that Hitchcock had added. He imagined Scottie as time's fool of love, finding it impossible to live with memory without falsifying it, inventing a double for Madeleine in another dimension of time, a zone that would belong only to him, and from which he could decipher the indecipherable story that had begun at Golden Gate when he had pulled Madeleine out of San Francisco Bay, when he had saved her from death before casting her back to death. Or was it the other way around?[4]

Hitchcock invented nothing. Not even the tower. On an earlier visit Hitchcock had seen the Mission with a higher tower, torn down in 1949. He recreated it on film.

The film Marker remembered was his own:

They walk. They look at the trunk of a redwood tree covered with historical dates. She pronounces an English name he doesn't understand. [Hitchcock?]....[5]
Here I was born and there I died. It was only a moment for you. You took no notice.
Downwardness in Hitchcock's movies is almost always associated with an image that suggests infernal regions, the land of the dead.... When [Scottie] next follows Madeleine the descent becomes still more marked: she goes down ten hills before she parks in front of Scottie's flat. After they begin to wander together the scenes have a fragrance of death about them. Among the redwoods of John Muir Forest Madeleine briefly disappears again.[6]

The camera's fascination with place dictates *Vertigo*'s visual surface. Publicized in part as a travel movie, San Francisco itself played a leading role. Structured on the themes of trailing and wandering, *Vertigo* takes its audience on a tour through and over the city, (the panorama that establishes the second half of the film, one of the most coldly elegant urban images in cinema). But if *Vertigo*'s San Francisco puts on a slightly off-putting face in overview, its interiors are irresistibly alluring, fixed in Marker's "spiral of time," confounding the viewer's nostalgia for that once-sophisticated city with its characters' insistence on more distant and irretrievable pasts.

Chris Marker's obsession with *Vertigo's* obsession, the *mise-en-abyme* of time, is echoed in Douglas Gordon's 24*-Hour Psycho* (1993), one of a number of contemporary artists who have seen the anti-naturalism of Hitchcock's later films (*Vertigo*'s scenography, costuming, and gestures are as stylized as Kabuki) as a provocation to even further intervention, though more often in the realm of the spatial rather than the temporal frame: Pierre

Huyghe's *Remake* (1994-95) or Cindy Bernard's Ask *the Dust* (1989-1992).

Many of the artistic interventions in *Vertigo* place the artist or the artist's creations *in media res*, not so much inside looking out, but inside being *looked at*.

I said that my ambition in life was to be a bedroom painter. Once someone asked, "What bedroom?" Without thinking I answered, "The bedrooms in Alfred Hitchcock's Vertigo.*"...Scottie's bedroom is the site of one of the most perverse love scenes in any movie. He carries "Madeleine" to his bed while she, Judy, pretends to be unconscious. It could only be suggested by her drying clothes, the shadowy lighting and warm atmosphere. Later in Judy's hotel room Scottie is intimate with her again only after she sacrifices her identity. Even while they make love Scottie cannot distinguish the real woman from his fantasy.*[7]

With the exception of Chris Marker, very few people have been more deeply engaged with *Vertigo* than Victor Burgin.

"When I first read a short essay by Freud called 'A Special Type of Choice of Object Made by Men' I was struck by the similarities between the syndrome of male desire Freud describes and the pattern of behavior Scottie exhibits in Hitchcock's film: The first condition determining the choice of love-object by the type of man described in Freud's essay is that the woman should already be attached to some other man – husband, fiancée, or friend. Scottie falls in love with the woman he is hired to investigate, the wife of an old college friend. The second precondition is that the woman should be seen to be of bad repute sexually: Madeleine, the college friend's wife, suffers from a fixated identification with a forbear whose illicit love-affair, and illegitimate child, brought her to tragic ruin. The type of man described by Freud is, "invariably moved to rescue the object of his love, and

prominent among the rescue fantasies of such men in the phantasm of rescue from water." Finally, Freud observes, "the lives of men of this type are characterized by a repetition of passionate attachments of this sort…each an exact replica of the other"….[8]

Power and freedom. Coupled together, these two words are repeated three times in Vertigo. *First, at the twelfth minute by Gavin Elster ('freedom' underlined by a move to a close-up) who, looking at a picture of Old San Francisco, expresses his nostalgia to Scottie…a nostalgia for a time when men – some men at least – had 'power and freedom.' Second, at the thirty-fifth minute, in the bookstore, where 'Pop' Liebel explains how Carlotta Valdez's rich lover threw her out yet kept her child: 'Men could do that in those days. They had the power and the freedom….' And finally at the hundred and twenty-fifth minute-and fifty-first second to be precise – but in reverse order (which is logical, given we are now in the second part, on the other side of the mirror) by Scottie himself when, realizing the workings of the trap set by the now free and powerful Elster, he says, a few seconds before Judy's fall – which for him will be Madeleine's second death – 'with all his wife's money and all that freedom and power….' Just try telling me these are coincidences.*[9]

Keep me safe.

Through all of the attention that *Vertigo* received in the overlapping worlds of cinema and the fine arts during the past forty years, Kim Novak's contribution to *Vertigo* was largely unacknowledged until very recently. In the exhibition catalogue *Vertigo*, curated and edited by Christian Leigh, Novak is mentioned by name fewer than five times in 125 pages of texts by 27 writers and critics, many of them prominent feminists.[10] Only one text focuses on Novak, Octavio Zaya's anecdotal tale of his absence. (James Stewart is discussed often – he *is* Scottie, while it seems from these readings that Madeleine / Judy wasn't played by anyone). In the saga of *Vertigo*'s rehabilitation from mid-level Hitchcock thriller to its present exalted position in nearly every critic's pantheon, each creative collaborator, both in front of and behind the camera has received serious attention except the actress whose image dominates the screen throughout the film and emerges, in the second part, as its protagonist. Her absence speaks volumes about the degree to which she was a victim of her own studio's publicity – and of Hitchcock's. For decades most critics, except the most perceptive, accepted Hitchcock's version of Novak's contribution, which was as self-serving as all of his judgments.

Like Godard and Antonioni, Hitchcock often preferred to use the most wooden actors and actresses – exploiting their discomfort as an element of suspense. The plausibility of Scottie's obsession, and much of the audience's willingness to entertain it, depends in large part on the seeming artlessness of Kim Novak's performance. She wasn't Hitchcock's first choice for the role; he preferred an icier blonde, but under his direction Novak's' vulnerability and sensuality were romanticized, *i.e.*, eroticized to a pitch far beyond what Hitchcock had been able to achieve with his other leading actresses.

The casting of Kim Novak in this role seems to me inspired, and gives her her most memorable role. The featurelessness of her presence and nonexistence of her acting allow full play to one's perversity; the lax voluptuousness of her smooth body – which Hitchcock insists on as upon no other of his heroines, in the scene in which she is wrapped in a sheet after her leap into San Francisco Bay – declaims perfect pliancy.[12]

Robin Wood initially disagreed. In his first reading of *Vertigo* he cited Novak's "occasional inadequacy" as "the film's only blemish."

Her performance as Madeleine, lovingly molded by Hitchcock, is flawless, but there are moments when one wants more inwardness from Judy…one becomes uncomfortably aware of the director behind the camera telling her "Now you do this…Now you do that…."[12]

Having drawn the wrong conclusion from a correct premise, Wood reversed himself in his revised 1989 edition of *Hitchcock's Films.*

I now see this [critique of Novak's performance] *as one of the* [earlier] *book's major critical blunders. Whatever Hitchcock's original casting choices (he wanted Vera Miles for the role)* Vertigo *as we have come to know it is unimaginable without Novak. One can even assert that…the film is* about *her…Richard Lippe…argues, from a feminist viewpoint, that Novak's star persona is centered upon an uncertainty as to her identity….*[13]

Lippe was responding to the critical perception, widely held at the time, that Kim Novak "couldn't act." His reply was worthy of Foucault: What, then, he inquired, *is* screen acting? Is it the same as acting in the legitimate theatre, or is it something different and particular to the cinema? His conclusion is close to Stanley Cavell's: that the great "film stars" inhabit their characters, merging their own "star" persona into their roles?

If this is cinema acting, then Kim Novak brought an unsurpassed and disquieting mixture of voluptuousness and vulnerability to her on-screen selves, and never more perfectly than as Madeleine Elster and Judy Barton.

The other perception that obscured Novak's importance was the idea that she was merely an object, something manufactured in the Columbia Studios star mill to replace Rita Hayworth and compete with Marilyn Monroe. Always the gentleman, the legendary Harry Cohn boasted to *Time* magazine, "If you wanna bring me your wife or your aunt, we'll do the same for them." If Cohn was right then another possible reading of *Vertigo* is available: as an on-screen metaphor of the creation of Kim Novak's "star" persona.

Jean-Luc Godard once said in discussing the possible 'readings' of a film that Vertigo *could be read as a documentary on "Kim Novak." Specifically, he was referring to the fact that the film is a document of her physical presence but…applies equally as a comment on the film's use of her star image.*[14]

If I let you change me, will that do it? If I do what you tell me will you love me?

[1] Robin Wood, "*Vertigo*" (1965), in *Hitchcock's Films Revisited* (New York: Columbia University Press, 1989).

[2] Stanley Cavell, *The World Viewed: Reflections on the Ontology of Film* (Cambridge: Harvard University Press, 1971).

[3] Gus Blaisdell, unpublished/untitled text, Interviews and manuscripts, Paris and Albuquerque, 1995-97.

[4] *Sans Soleil* (dir. Chris Marker, 1983).

[5] *La Jetée* (dir. Chris Marker, 1962).

[6] Leslie Brill, "I Look Up, I Look Down," in *The Hitchcock Romance* (Princeton: Princeton University Press, 1988).

[7] David Reed, *Two Bedrooms In San Francisco* (San Francisco, Walter and McBean Gallery, San Francisco Art Institute, 1992).

[8] Victor Burgin, *The Bridge* (1984), reproduced in *Passages* (Villeneuve d'Ascq: Musée d'Art Moderne Villeneuve d'Ascq, 1991).

[9] Chris Marker, "A Free Replay (notes on Vertigo)" *Positif* (June 1994).

[10] Christian Leigh, ed., *Vertigo* (Salzburg: Edition Thaddaeus Ropac, 1991).
[11] *Op. cit.*
[12] *Op. cit.*
[13] *Ibid.*
[14] Richard Lippe, "Kim Novak: A Resistance To Definition," *Cine-Action!* (Dec. 1986).

This text was published in Slavica Perkovic, *Vertigo* (Walther König, Cologne, 2012).

Additional Bibliography

Publications:

Pierre Boileau and Thomas Narcejac, *Vertigo* (London: Hutchinson, 1956).
Kerry Brougher, *: Art and Film Since 1945: Hall Of Mirrors* (New York: The Monacelli Press, 1996).
Robert E. Kapsis, *Hitchcock: The Making of a Reputation* (Chicago: University of Chicago Press, 1992).
Larry Kleno, *Kim Novak On Camera* (London: Gazelle Book Services, 1981).
Walter Raubicheck & Walter Srenbick, eds., *Hitchcock's Rereleased Films: From* Rope *to* Vertigo (Detroit: Wayne State University Press Detroit, 1991).
Slavoj Zizek, ed. *Everything you Always Wanted To Know About Lacan (But Were Afraid to Ask Hitchcock)* (London: Verso, 1992).

Television:

"Bernard Hermann" ARTE, Munich, 1997

Special Thanks To:
Mr. Dominique Bertrand, Paris
Mr. Gus Blaisdell, Albuquerque
Ms. Fabienne Galette, Paris
Mr. Jean-Claude Moinot, University of Paris VIII
Mr. Stephen Nash, Director, Palace of the Legion of Honor, San Francisco
Mr. David Reed, New York
Mr. Christophe Schifferli, SCT Communications, Zurich
Dr. Hubertus v. Amelunxen, Kiel
Ms. Connie Wirtz, Stephen Wirtz Gallery, San Francisco

MICHELINA

The artist had long grey hair and often ran his hands through his hair. He always smoked a cigarette while he drew and, if the drawing was going well and it was what he wanted, he never took the cigarette out of his mouth. It would go out on its own without his ever noticing. But if he took it out, put it out, lit another, it meant the drawing wasn't what he wanted. And then, he had a very particular way of dressing. He had really nice shirts and really colorful scarves and handkerchiefs, red or blue. He wore checkered shirts, in blues and greens, and, usually, beige pants. And he always wore clogs, never shoes. I hardly ever saw him in shoes.

When we started the pose, he hardly ever spoke, and he never told me what position to take. I was always the one who'd choose. He'd watch me and then he'd say: "Stay like that, don't move, that's a good position." And then he'd start to draw. While he was drawing, he never spoke, he never said a word. He'd only tell me – if I moved – to be still. He'd just look at me, and that was what was so striking because he no longer saw me as a person but as something to draw. It wasn't me anymore; it was like looking at a vase or a flower. Sometimes instead of just saying lift up or lower your hand, he'd just come over and move it. And if I asked, "What do I have to do?" he'd just say, "Nothing, just stay still." That's all he'd say. He didn't talk while he was drawing. He was always silent. He moved his hands a lot, he smoked, he observed, he drew. It was nice, but when he drew, I didn't exist. I don't remember him ever speaking to me, he hardly ever said anything.

He'd talk to me later, during the breaks, when he'd say: "You're tired. Maybe we should stop for a while." That's when he'd say: "OK. Let's talk." Or he'd read me stories, stories he liked, or he'd tell me about things he'd seen, or he'd say: "Look how beautiful this picture is." He'd show me catalogues of painters he liked, or he'd speak to me in English and he'd say: "Today we're going to have a conversation in English so you'll learn to speak a little better," something I never have. Then, he'd sing me arias from operas. I really liked listening to him sing Don Giovanni, and I'd ask him to repeat it over and over.

I would pose when I was at home on vacation. We lived near the Academy next to Porte Pinciana. My mother had an apartment there, and I usually posed in the afternoon around three, when the light was best, until around five. I'd go over, or he'd call to ask if I wanted to come over and pose. Sometimes I liked the idea, sometimes not so much because I would have rather gone outside to play. But then he'd say, "I have to finish something, I have to finish this drawing," and so I'd say, "OK, I'll come." But sometimes I really wanted to go because he had to finish telling me a story, or I'd liked what he'd done the day before and I wanted to continue to see how it would come out. So I'd leave the house, cross the garden and the wide path through the orange trees. I'd look at the stones on the ground, I'd look at the trees...Or sometimes I'd walk through the woods because I really liked going that way, passing unobserved. Then I'd reach the Academy and his door, and I'd knock, take the elevator, and go into his studio.

There was a beautiful door. I don't know if it's still like that but I remember it pink, light pink. And when I'd go into the studio, there was a really beautiful light that came through the window on the right. The sun lit up one whole part of the studio, while the other remained completely dark. He'd usually decide where to put the chair, where to put the armchair, where I had to sit, according to the light in the room. What I remember is that, when I opened the door, there was always this ray of sunlight that came in and lit up an entire part of the room. Then, there was a bed off to one side, there were green sofas, pink armchairs, and a strange chair that was half wood half velvet. It was a peculiar sort of chair, dark green, where he'd usually have me sit for drawings, or he'd choose an armchair, or the bed. It depended a bit on the position, on the drawing he was making.

The artist had two studios, one where he drew and prepared his paintings. He never had me pose in front of a canvas; I posed in front of a canvas maybe two or three times the whole time. He usually made preliminary drawings, the drawings he needed for his paintings. I spent most of my time in the studio where he made his drawings, which didn't smell like paint. It was a studio that smelled more like flowers; there was a strong scent of lime, I smelled that a lot. In the other studio, instead, in the one where he painted, where he practically never let anybody in, there was always a really strong smell of paint. It was a strange sort of place, a place where an alchemist might prepare formulas. It always made me think…when I went there…it made me really curious because it made me think of someone making something magical, something very special that nobody was supposed to see or was only supposed to see once it was finished. He prepared strange formulas, colors he mixed, things no one was supposed to know.

It was really his world. And I felt – really strongly – that he didn't want outsiders to see how he began a painting or everything he did in front of a canvas. It was completely different from when he made his drawings. When he was drawing, he was much more relaxed; there were other people, I was there, my sister was there. When he was in front of a painting, he always began alone and he never wanted…It was as if he was ashamed to show it, to show it to people who weren't involved.

I never met the artist's other models, except for my sister, with whom I posed a few times. He spoke about a few of them, but I never asked him anything because I really wasn't very interested. When I saw the paintings or the other drawings, I always found a resemblance between me and all the other models. There was always something we all had in common, I can't say what it was – a detail, a glance. Sometimes I had the impression of finding myself in paintings he had made much earlier.

When we'd finished posing, usually around 5 o'clock, the housekeeper would come to tell us tea was ready, and so we always finished work by going to tea. We'd go upstairs. The rest of the family was there. It was a real ritual, a ritual that was repeated practically every time. It was always somewhat the same. Tea was really important to them, and the way it was served was special. There were cookies, cookies he had brought in from a bar, from a bakery near the Villa, which tasted like lemon and were incredibly good. They were something that, well…just before I'd finish posing I'd always think that I was happy because it was almost time for tea and for the cookies I liked so much. There was this German woman who made really good pastries. I'd always go for the sweets. The tea ceremony lasted awhile, about an hour. Toward the end, I would start to get tired and think it might be time for me leave, to go home.

The tea ceremony was something really important for him

because he'd traveled, he'd been to Japan a lot too, and he really liked doing it. He would go and change, and he often put on a kimono. So it was truly an important moment of the day; his whole family was there and there were all these special rites. At the beginning, I was really curious. I watched how they served the tea and everything that was happening around me. Then after awhile, it seemed like it lasted a little too long, and I preferred to leave.

When I started to pose, I was still really young so I didn't really know who this artist was. I didn't know how important he was. Everyone had told me he was very well known in the world of art, but I'd never seen anything and I didn't know who he was...So I discovered...I'd never seen the paintings...so I discovered a world I hadn't known. And then, little by little, I started to get to know him better. I posed for him for several years, and I became a part of his family, we were all together a lot. And then I started to understand that he was a rather important person, someone who was well known because a lot of other people came to see him, they came to tea. He was always meeting with people, intellectuals, artists...There were always new people who'd come by to see him, to talk to him. And so I'd listen. At the beginning, I was bored, but bit by bit, I grew more interested in what they were saying. I met film directors. At the beginning I even met Fellini, who took me to see how a film was made. And then other artists and other people came by, and it was always really interesting to see how he related to them, what he said. Everyone was there to listen to him; it was as though he had the ability to attract everyone's attention.

One thing he taught me was to see...to know to look, always, at beautiful things, to stand in front of a painting, to love painting…to stand in front of painting and to see it a bit through his eyes, through what he'd told me…through what he'd told me when we went to see exhibitions and when we looked at catalogues.

I started posing when I was young and I posed for several years, I lived through the moment of transition from childhood to adolescence. At the time, it was something I lived differently. I looked at the drawings and saw my appearance changing. There was a physical evolution. I didn't really understand what he was representing. Now, now that I'm older and I look at the drawings in a more detached way, I sometimes don't recognize myself. There are poses that are really sexually charged, a charge I can't find now. I think they're very particular moments, moments one lives at that age or in that particular phase of life.

The fact that he used the same models or models that looked alike was one of his traits. I can't say why he always looked for a certain type of woman – of girl – that always had something in common. I don't know exactly what it was that bound all the models to me or to my sister or to the others.

What always seems strange is thinking that there are a lot of people looking at paintings of me, looking at me, and sometimes I wonder what they're thinking when they look at these drawings. The relationship between a painter and his model is always something very special. I think that the role of the model is fundamental, or at least mine with respect to this artist. A really strong bond is formed and perhaps a certain dependence. The model always depends on the artist, and the artist depends a bit on the model. It's something quite unique that's difficult to describe. There's something that binds you and there are feelings that take root. He tries to find in you…he tries to find things in you that he can represent, aspects…not only physical aspects. He tries to transcribe who you are or were, and it depends a lot on the model whether they are revealed or not.

When I go to an opening or an exhibition of the artist, there's always someone who recognizes me or who sees me as the artist's model. There are people in whom I sense curiosity, others a morbid curiosity, others somewhat less. They always want…they try to look at me, looking at the drawings…they want to know what danger…what's behind them. Or they start to ask me questions or to look at me strangely…Sometimes I'm flattered they recognize me. I think that, no matter what, I'll be immortal, I'll live on in his works…A lot of people see the eroticism in these paintings in a controversial light. I often meet people that don't like this artist, that find him strange, that find his sensuality or his eroticism somewhat peculiar. I always think that perhaps they don't see the painting, that they don't see the drawings, the same way I do. For me, the artist is someone who wanted to express an important moment…an important moment of passage from innocence to eroticism, from childhood to becoming an adult.

It's difficult to say what of this experience remains with me today. What bothers me, or what I thought about even then and still I carry with me, is always what others think…what others think of me. And so it always depends entirely on who…on the interest I have in who is asking me certain questions. It's an experience that leaves with you something, that leaves its marks, and you're always there. It weakens you somehow because you're always wondering what others think of you. I live it with greater detachment now.

I was born in France and I spent a few years in Paris. We

traveled a lot because my father had come to France from Italy because he had a company. My mother had joined him some time later. My two sisters were born in Italy, but I was born in Paris, more exactly in a small town near Paris. We traveled a lot then, and we moved a lot. We spent some time there before moving to Paris, then from Paris to Versailles. I remember very little about my childhood in France. I lived there until I was 8 or 9 years old. My mother tongue is French, so when I arrived in Italy, I couldn't speak and didn't understand a word of Italian. Of my schooling [in France], I have really vague memories of preschool and of the last house where I lived with my mother and my father and one of my sisters because the other one, the oldest one, was studying in Italy. We lived in this really big house surrounded by a yard, where, I remember, we were always riding our bicycles and spending our days. It was a two-storey house, and what I remember is that my room was on the upper floor and that we could even go straight from the garden to bed and that was really fun. I had an aunt who came to visit a lot and lived with us often, and I was really attached to her. There was a woman who lived nearby, a neighbor who was a really good friend of my mother's. She had children and grandchildren, and she had a daughter who lived in Italy. When my father died, my mother didn't know what to do and she decided to go back to Italy. She spoke about it with her friend, our neighbor, who told her that her daughter was a fellow at Villa Medici and, if she [my mother] was interested, she could go to work at the Villa. I remember these things really vaguely but my mother always used to tell me about them.

When we moved to Italy, we sold everything. We kept the house for a while, until a few years ago actually, but we brought all our belongings with us. My recollection of this move from Paris to Rome and Villa Medici is really vague. My first impression when I arrived at this place, the very first time I saw it, it seemed so big, so huge, the garden was enormous with respect to my garden in France. It was like a labyrinth, a place to play, where I spent my time. The first few days I spent all my time running around this garden, I took my bicycle and rode around or played hide-go-seek. There was a dog that belonged to the Villa caretaker, a really nice German shepherd. You might say he was my first friend at Villa Medici. I spent most of my days running after or playing hide-go-seek with him. I'd go down the walkways and I'd hide, and after awhile he'd show up and would begin to run around madly...The Villa was impressive, it was gigantic, and I felt really small in respect to this monument, in respect to such a big, such a classical building, which was even a bit cold but, at the same time, filled with the warmth of the people living there. What I still remember about the garden are the scents, and the walkway through the orange trees, a walkway full of trees and bushes...At that time the bushes were much larger, and the garden wasn't anything like it is now. It seemed truly... if someone wanted to hide...for a child...it was a really fun game because the bushes were really big and they were everywhere. I spent my afternoons playing there. And, then, I was only at Villa Medici on my vacations, in the summer and at Christmas, because, when we arrived in Italy, my sister and I went to study in Florence. My mother sent us to a boarding school there. My sister went back before me because she was really attached to my mother, but I stayed on through junior high school and I only came back to Rome, to Villa Medici, on my vacations. My sister met the artist when she went back to Villa Medici, and he asked her to model, to pose for him. When I arrived at the Villa, one day when I'd come back on vacation, I was really curious and I asked my sister if I could come with her when she posed and see what she did.

My first impression, I remember, was this door. The door opened and there was this studio, this huge room. There were even frescoes on the ceiling, and there were objects in the room: there were armchairs, chairs, lots of sheets of paper and lots of pencils. My sister said, "Look, this is what you do," and she took a pose, a pose the artist suggested. I sat down in a corner to watch what was happening. She didn't move. He kept looking at her and drew and drew without stopping. He had a cigarette in his mouth the whole time and he smoked continuously. But when he was drawing he couldn't take his eyes off his model, so the cigarette stayed lit until the end. The session lasted about an hour. I was intrigued and I wanted to do the same thing. He asked me if I wanted to try and I said: "Yes, why not." I too wanted to have this experience and imitate what my sister was doing. So I said yes.

The first time it was a bit complicated. It's difficult to remain still, you want to move, you want to scratch yourself. When he said, "Stay like that," I understood I couldn't move anymore, I couldn't move anything. It's a really strange sensation, because the moment someone tells you to stay still is the moment in which you want to move, to get up, or walk around. It's the moment in which your foot or your arm falls asleep, or you want to run your hands through your hair. So you start thinking about other things, you start letting your mind wander, you start thinking about dreaming, making up stories, or you invent situations...trying to stay as still as possible. I remember that, staying still like that, you have thousands of sensations, you feel scents or colors, whatever is around you, much more intensely. The first time, I even remember being a little cold. At the beginning I thought it was a bit boring and that I didn't really like it, but when it was over and I saw the result, I felt really flattered. It seemed impossible that he was really so good, that he'd managed to draw me so well, that that was really me, and that I'd been able to keep still that whole time. While he drew, I often looked at him and I have to say that I found him…sometimes he scared me a bit, sometimes not so much. I found…I found him physically imposing. He had long white hair, and he often passed his hands through his hair. He had really beautiful blue eyes and a really penetrating gaze. Most of all he had really beautiful hands and a really particular way of holding a pencil or a cigarette. The artist always fascinated me. I found him, physically, from a certain point of view, handsome, especially when I spent time posing. I looked at him as he looked at me, and I had strange sensations because I was often attracted to him, it was… it was always a conflicting emotion, a conflicting situation. What fascinated me about him was his intelligence, his culture. Whatever I asked him, he always knew everything about everything. And for me it was as if I had a talking encyclopedia in front of me. This is something that has stayed with me with respect to other people I meet. It's what I always look for, to see what I can learn from what they know. He was an endless source from which I could take anything, and this is what fascinated me the most, it's what attracted me most. After some time, when our relationship had gotten closer, when we knew each other better, once, he took me…we took a trip together. He had to go to Tuscany so we left together, traveling by car with his whole family. It was really fun to see him – this once – in a different way, other than behind his sheet of paper, behind his painting. I saw him as another person, someone who was actually there, or who was driving, or could actually drive a car. He always did things in such an aristocratic way, it was strange to see him as a normal person just like everyone else. Along the way we stopped in Ovieto, we saw other small cities and he took me to see beautiful churches. And then in Florence, when we arrived in Florence, he took me to see the monuments, and he helped me discover the most beautiful part of the city.

I stopped…I stopped posing when I was older, when I was 16, because I didn't want to spend my time that way anymore. It took up too much time, it took entire afternoons and I had to study too. At a certain moment, I said stop. It seemed like that phase was over. I was the one who decided, and I told him I didn't want to pose anymore. At the beginning, it was a bit complicated for him because he had things he needed to finish, but later he understood. And then he moved to another city and it was much easier.

CODA

In 1998 I was invited by Frederic Lefever to present my work at the Académie de France à Rome – the Villa Medici. I felt honored to be invited. During the course of my short visit I learned the unspoken dynamic of the Villa. The pensioners were offered residence for one year; directors for three.

The continuity of management was the responsibility of the Italian employees of the Villa, most of whom had worked there all their lives; many for generations. First in seniority was Massimiliano, the barman; his predecessors had held the same position, a hereditary treasure, since 1848. The gardeners were relative newcomers: their family had held those positions only since World War I.

A similar hereditary system obtained in the executive positions. The executive secretary to the director was Michela Terreri, and her mother had held that position before. In fact, Michela and her sister had grown up, in great part, in the Villa, an almost fairy-tale Eden perched on the Trinità del Monte overlooking the city. She and her sister had modeled for Balthus during his legendary directorship of the Villa in the 1960s and 70s. We were introduced briefly as I was leaving the Villa to return to Paris.

A few months later I was approached by Laurence Bossé and Hans-Ulrich Obrist, who had been asked by the new director, of the Villa, Bruno Racine, to organize a series of the summer exhibitions on the themes of *The City*, *The Garden*, and *Memory*. They invited me to participate.

After a very long period of negotiations Michela agreed to make a work with myself and Slavica Perkovic, an audio recording in which she spoke of her early adolescent life in the Villa and of course, of Balthus. The work was exhibited that summer in an empty painting studio.

The work was an audio piece, and it was to all of our good fortunes that Michela Terreri held an advanced degree in art history, was a cultivated and intelligent person, and, of importance to an audio work, had a wonderful voice.

She told me that she was always indebted to Balthus and to his wife for introducing her to the world of art and they remained friends until his death in 2001.

The preceding text is a transcription from an audio installation in the exhibition *La Ville, Le Jardin, La Mémoire: 1999 La Mémoire,* Académie de France à Rome, Villa Medici, Rome, Italy, 1999, and features an audio interview with Michela Terreri who is the primary of the three co-authors of this piece, along with Slavica Perkovic and Lewis Baltz.

TOSCA

"As all History must converge to Opera in the Italian Style..."
Thomas Pynchon, *Mason & Dixon*[1]

Initially I had proposed two projects for this summer's exhibition at the Villa Medici, *Michelina* and *Tosca.* I thought of them as related projects, as both center on women whose lives, or part of whose lives, turn around art. Both projects were accepted but because of time constraints we were only able to complete *Michelina.*

Tosca has always held a great fascination for me and in this I'm hardly unique: it's a favorite of millions who enjoy, but are not specialists in opera. At its debut *Tosca* was dismissed by music critics as an overwrought, shabby melodrama, and there is a considerable body of critical opinion that persists in that view. *Tosca*'s defenders have usually resorted to the (deeply flawed) argument that the opera's continued popular success is proof in itself of its greatness – or at least of its validity. Leaving that debate aside, my absorption is with the almost prescient modernity of its theme and of Tosca's antagonist, the loathsome Baron Scarpia: quintessential secret policeman and a study in the pathology of power.

Scarpia belongs more to us and to our century than to his own; a thoroughly modern man. His pretext is the suppression of terrorism, his weapon is terror, and his subtext is the gratification of his personal appetites. He is not the world's first secret policeman, but stands near the head of a line of murderers and blackmailers whose descendants include Beria, Himmler, and J. Edgar Hoover.

It is my intention to film the sites of several scenes from *Tosca* as they are today, in a Rome transformed over the past two centuries from a site of sublime glories and heinous crimes into a tourist attraction and shopping mall. My initial request to film in the Villa Farnese (Act II) was refused out of hand, despite the personal intervention of Bruno Racine, whose friendship with the Ambassador predated his posting to Rome. Of the three sites of Tosca, the Villa Farnese remains as it was in Scarpia's time, a functioning embassy of an important foreign power and, as such, a security zone. What I will make of the Villa Farnese I will have to do by indirection, using pre-existing footage and photographs.[2]

The Chiesa Sant' Andrea della Valle (Act I) and the Castel Sant' Angelo (Act III) are, in varying degrees, public places, and I believed that with a bit of mediation it would be possible to receive an authorization to film there.

Timelines are easy enough to draw, but I like the symmetry nevertheless: the historic event loosely depicted in *Tosca* took place in Rome in late 1799; Puccini wrote the opera in 1899 and it debuted in Rome in January, 1900; I hope to make my film in January 2000.

The audio element (which, of course, would dominate) will be taken from various early recorded performances. I have access to the music library of the Bibliothèque Nationale in Paris and, if necessary, to the Biblioteca nazionale in Rome.

It was not my intention to re-film the entire work, but only a few selected scenes. To attempt more would be over ambitious and probably not very interesting. If this work did go ahead, it would be with the consent and technical support of the Musée d'Art Moderne de la Ville de Paris and the French Academy in

Rome, with the idea that it be first screened in next summer's edition of *La Ville, Le Jardin, La Mémoire.*[3]

[1] Thomas Pynchon, *Mason & Dixon* (New York: Henry Holt and Co., 1997).

[2] A few years later I had the pleasure of dining with Patrick Talbot, newly appointed director of the École Nationale Supérieure de la Photographie in Arles. We'd met several years before in New York when he was the cultural attaché at the French consulate. He said that he had been in Rome in the late 90s, as cultural attaché to the Embassy. I laughed and said, "Oh, so you're the *functionaire* who refused my project." He didn't remember so I told him more or less what I just related here. He said that the request had never reached him; had it he would have enthusiastically accepted, and I believe him. If there's a moral it is, I suppose, that one can never underestimate the influence of sheer human error in the affairs of one's life.

[3] *La Ville, Le Jardin, La Mémoire: 2000 Jardin,* Académie de France à Rome, Villa Medici, Rome, Italy, 2000.

Author's note: "Tosca" was written in 1999 and was all that I could salvage out of (what turned out to be an unnecessarily) frustrating period when I was briefly at the American Academy in Rome and was trying to secure authorizations to film on the sites of *Tosca,* nearly everybody's favorite opera.

Notes on Thomas Ruff

THOMAS RUFF AND THE *KULTURWUNDER*

The 1980s witnessed the high watermark of German influence in contemporary art. The pillars of the *Kulturwunder* were Neo-Expressionist painting, and its antithesis, the austere and conceptually driven works of Bernd and Hilla Becher and their more gifted students. Compared with the earlier radicalism of Joseph Beuys it must be said that both practices were studiously conservative. When the German tidal wave subsided at the end of the decade only the painters Baselitz, Kiefer, Polke and Richter, and the Bechers and their students, Thomas Ruff, Andreas Gursky, Thomas Struth, and Axel Hütte, remained.

Inscribed in a tradition as old as Dürer, the Bechers' life work has been the compilation of an exhaustive typology of common architectural forms; though not strictly speaking conceptual artists, their photographic practice was well suited to accompany Conceptualism in its researches. In opposition to the more visceral threads of the German cultural tapestry, the Bechers' heritage was precision, rigor, and distance. Thomas Ruff was their initial beneficiary, and, as such, was instrumental in colonizing the cultural space (audience, market, and critical discourse) that he and his former schoolmates presently occupy.

THOMAS RUFF AND HIS WORK

Ruff's first widely-seen and still best-known works, the *Portraits*, (anonymous headshots enlarged to over two meters high) flirted with the unachieved Minimalist ideal of the work of art with only one quality. The *Portraits* posed the question if scale, *by itself*, is enough to transform photo-booth snapshots into art; the *a priori* answer would seem to be no, but the empirical answer was a resounding Yes. The *Portraits* demonstrated the assertion that changes in magnitude can become changes in kind – they were not only bigger but fundamentally different from what they were before; paradoxically the subjects' faces seem to dematerialize before the viewer's eyes. Extremes shifts of scale have been an enduring concern in Ruff's work from the minuscule *Newspaper Photos* to his recent gargantuan, "Heartfield" photomontages.

From the series *Houses* and *Stars*, through the *Newspaper Photos*, *Night*, *3-D*, and *Retouch*, Ruff has continued to interrogate the possibilities of well-known genres and techniques of photographic representation, always with a precision of rendering and an emotional neutrality that undermine the possibility of an anecdotal superficiality. Ruff's nominal subjects (and he insists on their nominality) are drawn from the banal: undistinguished buildings; stretches of the cosmos as seen through telescopes (Ruff is an keen amateur astronomer); newspaper photos; infra-red images of the kind seen through sniper sights made famous in the TV reportage of the Gulf War; "stereo" photographs; awkward found studio portraits. Ruff cites Flaubert's *Dictionnaire des idées reçues*, and his strategy recalls Jasper Johns' dictum, "things the mind already knows."

THOMAS RUFF AND ARCHITECTURE

A particularity of Ruff's artistic practice is his ongoing collaboration with the architects Herzog & de Meuron, breaking with a decades long banishment of "serious," (as opposed to found) architecture from "serious" (as opposed to commercial) photography. The estrangement came about, one could imagine, when self-conscious photographers, hoping to establish their own claims of authorship, refused to illustrate another artist's creation; or perhaps it was also when architects, or the more thoughtful among them, realized that the camera's glass eye could produce only an emblematic rendering of their complex efforts. Ruff's strategy was to photograph Herzog & de Meuron's buildings as though they were as anonymous as his *Häuser.* "I take a look at the building; I notice certain aspects of it and then I say, OK, this photograph is one exemplary view of the building – a view that basically enables you to recognize it...I'm not really concerned about finding the "right" representation of the building...I don't see that as my task."

THOMAS RUFF AND CRITICISM

Ruff's work can be most accurately spoken of in the vocabulary of formalism, which, before it became a curse-word, was originally defined (by Clement Greenberg) as the use of a medium to perform an auto-critique of its intrinsic, induplicable qualities, *i.e.*, an art which was first and foremost a meditation on the conditions of its own existence. It is exactly there that Thomas Ruff stakes his claim to our attention: his programmatic investigation of the genres and procedures presently available to photographic representation. In his compilation of a continually expanding inventory (or index or typology) of artistic strategies. Ruff has left the more "retinal" applications of his research to others.

THOMAS RUFF AND HIS COLLEAGUES

The two most prominent artists in the Becher School, Thomas Ruff and Andreas Gursky, are often compared, and the differences between them are instructive. Gursky is a photographer, born of photographers, who were themselves born of photographers. (Unlike other branches of the entertainment industry, dynasties are still relatively uncommon in the visual arts). Gursky operates from the same impulse that has traditionally motivated photographers: to make an aesthetic statement about something observed in the world. As such, Gursky is arguably the most skilled photographer of our time while Ruff's interests have always been elsewhere.

THOMAS RUFF IN PARIS

Ruff's work is controlled and controlling, addressing itself to a collective will to impose order on the chaos of experienced reality. Ruff photographs could be described as Apollonian, Classic, Northern and cerebral, so much so as to be emblematic of those stern and glacial virtues. On the occasion of Ruff's first retrospective exhibition on the European mainland – the only other was in Scandinavia – its should be interesting to see how Parisian audiences, themselves Dionysian, Romantic, Mediterranean, sensual, and habituated to both a lighter and sweeter artistic fare, will respond to Ruff's propositions. There is, after all, nothing in Ruff's work that asks to be liked. But there is much, not the least of which is Ruff's refusal to ingratiate, that provokes reflection and respect.

This text originally appeared as "Notes sur Thomas Ruff," in *L'Architecture d'Aujourd'hui*, no. 313 (October 1997). Editor's note: This text was published during the exhibition *Thomas Ruff* at the Centre National de la Photographie, Paris, France, 1997.

Velocity Piece #2 (Impact Run, 1969), Barry Le Va

Harald Szeemann has frequently gone on record to point out that there were only two periods of radical innovation in the visual arts in the 20th century, the years preceding WWI and, again, in the 1960s. If he's right it's not cheerful news, that most of us have spent most, or all, of our professional lives in a protracted mopping-up action.

Dealt a hand like that it's smarter, at my age, to play it very close to your vest. Otherwise, it sounds too much like Glory Days, when apples tasted sweeter and women's thighs were tighter, and yeah, yeah, yeah. Old fart talk. The problem is that Szeemann is *objectively* right.

Long ago and far away, much of the first-hand knowledge I had of contemporary art was acquired in the galleries of the then La Jolla Museum of Contemporary Art. At the time it was a great place to see contemporary art; probably still is. It was there that I saw my first works by Robert Irwin, Bruce Nauman, Mowry Baden, Chris Burden, and in 1970 an especially important work by Barry Le Va, *Velocity Piece #2 (Impact Run*, 1969).

Le Va's installation didn't offer much in the way of visual incidents: a few smudges at shoulder level on two facing walls of the room, maybe a fleck of blood, or maybe I just imagined the blood. An empty white room with a stereo audio tape of the artist running from wall to wall, hitting one wall, running back, hitting the opposite wall; runnin' till he couldn't run no more. The piece lasted 56 minutes.

I was luckier than I knew at the time. *Velocity Piece #2* was exhibited only twice, a year before at Ohio State University in a longer version (1 hour 43 minutes) and in the installation I saw in La Jolla. After 1970, Le Va never again reconstructed the work, though a number of later shows referenced it through documentation.

Velocity Piece #2 expanded my idea of the possibilities and obligations of art (in the historical determinist framework of that moment the possible was also the necessary). Even better, it confirmed my undoubtedly naive belief that art was a noble profession that would change the world by subtly changing our perceptions.

Le Va announced another idea of figuration, not as representation – another statue, another picture – but as an actual event, or its traces; the human body, not as the art's subject but as its material, like paint or metal. This was, I believe, somewhat before Acconci and Burden would develop this position in different ways.

When I saw *Velocity Piece #2* I didn't know Barry Le Va; in fact I knew nothing about him at all, other than this one work. I wasn't to meet him for another fifteen years, when a mutual friend, Don Dudley, introduced us in New York. I moved to Paris in 1985 and *Velocity Piece #2* followed into the collection of the Centre Pompidou, two blocks from my house. Small world.

Le Va's work changed, and, then again, hasn't. For a while, Le Va's work 'materialized' into something more redolent of sculpture; a few years ago he showed some of these pieces here in Paris, and *Artpress* was appreciative. More recently he's been working with collage. The constant that I see (other than intelligence) is a sense that whatever you experience in relation to his work, you are also made conscious of something else, outside the work, to which Le Va gives indexes and traces.

This text originally appeared in *Purple*, no. 5 (Summer 2000).

MIGROPOLIS

COMMON SENSE

Societies closed to immigration ossify. Societies overrun by immigration lose their sense of themselves as a polity. The only question is to determine how much immigration, and in which circumstances, is optimum for the health of the host society. This is easier said than done, and in the absence of a comprehensive population policy in the host country, nearly impossible. Capitalism, as always, exacerbates the problem as certain classes within the host society stand to benefit from immigration at the expense of other classes.

Until fairly recently, advocates of immigration were the boss classes, working tirelessly to drive down labor costs; anti-immigration policies favored the working classes and were, as such, progressive. These poles have been reversed.

The politics of immigration are complicated by questions of racism, post-colonial guilt, and broadly held European values concerning what are acceptable degrees of unemployment and the limits of the social contract. Underneath the rational discourse lurks the ugly *Id* of identity politics, against which traditional Judeo-Christian and Humanist ideas of justice and charity, as well as the saccharine antidote of multiculturalism proved ineffective.

What remains is no longer politics, but as Zizek claims, "biopolitics…a politics of fear…a frightened rallying of frightened men."

"This is why the big event – not only in Europe – in early 2006 was that anti-immigration politics 'went mainstream': the umbilical link that connected them to the far Right fringe parties was finally cut...The main parties now find it acceptable to stress that the immigrants are guests who have to accommodate themselves to the cultural values that define the host society – it is 'our country, love it or leave it."[1]

Although Zizek doesn't cite it, the highly mediatized rebellion in the Paris *banlieues* in late 2005 played a leading role in this hardening of attitudes, and not only in France, where it legitimized a move further right by the Gaullists. (Successful move, as the 2007 French elections proved with the election of hard-liner Nicholas Sarkozy and the hollowing out the ranks of Jean-Marie Le Pen's *Front National*, and wreaking a condign punishment on the Socialists for betraying their working class constituencies, both indigenous and immigrant.)

The *evenements* in Paris would hold little claim on the attention of other Europeans except insofar as they might mirror, or anticipate, a more general situation. Anyway, Italy is different kettle of fish, or so it seems.

IN ITALIA

For a host of reasons the burden of nationalism has rested far more lightly on the shoulders of Italians than it has on the populations of other large European states, often to the intense frustration of leaders who would have it otherwise. (A substantial part of the Fascist project in the 1920s was simply to indoctrinate Italians to see themselves as Italians.)

Over two millennia of barbarian invasions and settlement contributed to making Italian identity a rather fluid concept. On top of this rested the social realities of the new Italian state, which, plagued by structural poverty was an enormous exporter of people. (The United States was the major beneficiary of this exodus. It's estimated that in 1940 one Italian family in three had a relative of first cousin or closer living in the U.S., which might have contributed to the fact that during WWII Italian soldiers – who had served bravely under Rommel and on the Russian front – had so little heart to do battle with the Americans).

With its belated *Wirtschaftswunder* in the 1970s, Italy began to attract immigrants. Within a couple of decades Italy changed from exporter to importer of people. Italy, never a colonial power of real consequence, and just getting accustomed to experiencing a vibrant economy as a normal state of affairs, seemed, more than anything else, bemused by the presence of these strangers within its gates. The central government was predictably slow to respond; a bureau of immigration at the governmental level only came into existence in the early 1990s.

On one of my Italian voyages in the 1990's I recall seeing an issue of the *Corriere della Serra's* weekend magazine. On the cover, if I recall correctly, was a photograph of a black man wearing what appeared to be the ceremonial uniform of what I further surmised was an erstwhile all-lily-white Italian regiment. The photograph was in no way demeaning: the man resonated with martial dignity. But it was shocking in the context of an Italy whose notion of 'the other' had before been confined to an exacerbated form of the North-South rivalry common in many countries. As I stumbled through the article I recalled that the author cited the presence of a Philippine colony of 50,000 souls in Rome. (Why Philipinos? Why Rome?) A few weeks later, in Helsinki, the topic of immigration came up in a conversation with Lawrence Weiner; I mentioned this curious statistic and Weiner laughed and put it in perspective: "Fifty-thousand people? That's a rock concert!" Even now, more than a decade later, Italians seem no closer to arriving at a consensus of what constitutes 'The Other' and 'What is to be done' than they are to arriving at any other consensus. Though that might be changing.

BAD BAGS, BAD JOSS, BAD FAITH

Within the framework of Italian exceptionalism lies the specific question of Venetian exceptionalism. In Venice, where Venetian dialect is the *lingua franca*, the question of 'the Other' is closely and neatly drawn: it is the non-Venetian, and that includes Italians unlucky enough to be born outside the lagoon. On the other hand, as the seat of a maritime empire, Venice has traditionally hosted a large foreign community, both as visitors and as menials. When the Mediterranean was the ocean of trade the visitors were commercial travelers and the menials slaves. Now that the Mediterranean is the ocean of mass tourism the visitors are tourists and the menials low level functionaries in the 'Hospitality Industry,' which employs forty percent of the documented workers in Venice. Though exact numbers are difficult to confirm as so much of Venice's economy is under the table. Wolfgang Scheppe's *Migropolis* project is the first instance I know to acknowlege the relationship between tourism and immigration and to attempt to draw its broad outlines.

In a city of 60,000 inhabitants, with a tourist influx of over 20 million persons per year – mostly arriving between Easter and Bank Holiday – most immigrants are invisible. A large number are Eastern European women who enjoy a special work visa status in Italy as care givers to the infirm and the aged. Building construction employs many other immigrants of European origins, legally and otherwise.

The real sense of confrontation, the points of conflict between Venetians and non-Venetians are the sellers of counterfeit purses and bags who populate the streets around San Marco and Rialto, hawking ugly copies of ugly originals of Prada, Vuitton, etc. It's a hard buck, standing around all day, merchandise spread on a tarp for easy concealment and escape from the police, hustling in every European language passers-by who overwhelmingly ignore them. The resentments that they provoke in Venetian shopkeepers (who have their own pricey counterfeit rubbish to flog and don't relish competition) are in great degree racial: the 'bad bags' vendors are black, tall, often dressed in African garb: glaringly and irreducibly 'other'.

The authorities make a charade of policing the street vendors with sporadic 'surprise' raids. The police, in full dress regalia will start at one end of The Strada Nova and work their way to the other. Their presence is telegraphed by everything except trumpets. The bag vendors warn each other on their *telephonniis* and – surprise! – the police see no lawbreakers. The bag sellers fold up their wares in a tarp, duck into a side street, or a café, wait a few minutes, and resume work after the Keystone Cops have strutted past. (To see the humor of this, imagine it filmed in planographic view.)

A couple of years ago a nationwide law was passed, and widely advertised, that threatened to penalize the buyers of counterfeit bags with fines of up to 10,000 euros. It was rumored that the law was enforced once, in Verona perhaps, and a luckless tourist was fined 1,500 euros. The story may very well be apocryphal. In reality the authorities have no interest in stopping or controlling this traffic and its not entirely certain that they should.

Another group that has a negative visibility are the Chinese who in many cases come legally as investors rather than laborers. Any number of small enterprises are run, and well run, by Chinese proprietors, in Venice as elsewhere. The negative visibility factor enters when Chinese buy neighborhood bars, which had been hereditarily Venetian. The locals and the tourists expect to find a Venetian, or someone who can pass for Venetian, on the other side of the bar.

While both these non-European groups are highly visible in the workplace they otherwise pass nearly unseen in the city. This in itself seems eerie to Venetians.

CONCERNING THE ROLE OF POST-PHOTOGRAPHIC PHOTOGRAPHY

Photography, it's been often asserted (on a few occasions by the present author) is bankrupt. If that is so one need look no further than 1989 to find the date that it filed its Chapter 13. But, like airlines, 'Photography' (or better, 'photography') works at its highest level of efficiency when it is in receivership. If we think of it in this way, its easier to see how Wolfgang Scheppe and his collaborators picked up photography, examined it, dusted off the pieces most useful in their enterprise, and used them as elements in building *Migropolis.*

[1] Slavoj Zizek, *Robespierre: Virtue and Terror* (London and New York: Verso, 2007).

This text originally appeared in *Migropolis: Venice / Atlas of a Global Situation*, ed. Wolfgang Scheppe (Ostfildern: Hatje Cantz, 2010).

Meetings with Remarkable Men: John McLaughlin

I couldn't have been much younger than fourteen when I first saw a work by John McLaughlin. I know this because it was a painting made in 1959, a small oil sketch for a larger work that would go to the Los Angeles County Museum of Art. The painting was inscribed "to William Current", my mentor and himself a remarkable figure. McLaughlin gave it to him as thanks for his making slides of McLaughlin's works. Although Current's wife, Constance Counter, was a talented painter, none of her canvases were displayed in their home, only their collection of antique Chinese furniture and objects and the McLaughlin painting.

In 1961 William Current closed his failing camera shop. He and Connie sold nearly all of their possessions and moved to Santa Fe, New Mexico. William Current staked everything on this once in a lifetime effort to establish himself as a photographic artist. (He won his wager: within two years the Museum of Modern Art in New York had acquired and exhibited Current's work; in 1964 he received a Guggenheim Fellowship and in 1965 was given a solo exhibition at the Art Institute of Chicago.)[1]

Bill sold me the McLaughlin painting in Taos, New Mexico, in 1963. It was my companion as I moved around the United States and, in 1986, to Paris, and then Milan, where we parted company in 1989. I believe that at that time it was the first John McLaughlin painting in Italy; it may still be.

I've a very clear memory of my first impression of McLaughlin's work: I thought that the rigor, the simplicity and the sublime beauty of McLaughlin's vision was what the art of the present and future should be.

McLaughlin's work was highly respected in the region: he was the centerpiece of *Four Abstract Classicists*,[2] the landmark exhibition curated by Jules Langsner at the Los Angeles County Museum of Art in 1959, who coined the term "Hard Edge" painting to describe work the works in the exhibition. In a special California issue in 1962 *Life* magazine featured John McLaughlin and four other California artists; McLaughlin is posed with one of his canvases on a golf course, in full golfer's dress.

Between 1961 and 1969 I had completed high school, received a B.F.A. from the San Francisco Art Institute, successfully avoided military conscription, and was returning to Southern California for graduate studies at the Claremont Graduate School.

Los Angeles in the late 60s had given me a new set of art heroes to accompany John McLaughlin in my personal pantheon: Ed Ruscha, (*Twenty-Six Gasoline Stations*), Robert Irwin (the discs) and Barry LeVa (*Velocity Run 2*) immediately, and others very soon after. I was convinced not only that this was what the art of the present and future should be but also that it was what the art of the present and future *must* be. Along the way I had become a determinist.

In 1969 I decided to return to my detested birthplace, Southern California, for two connected reasons: the clear and obvious fact that all of the new thinking about art in California seemed to be coming from L.A.,[3] and because an old friend, Tom Holste – who had just completed the first year of his M.F.A. at Claremont, encouraged me to apply to the graduate program there.[4]

Tom Holste, a friend since my senior year in high school, had survived the psychedelic revolution to become a committed and sophisticated painter; the subject of his Master's thesis was John McLaughlin.

Holste spent hundreds of hours at McLaughlin's home, interviewing him about his philosophy of painting, which developed out of his contact with Zen Buddhist art during the years he'd lived in Japan.

Unlike most Westerners in the thrall of Asia, McLaughlin left the imagery and calligraphy for others, concentrating on the experience of pure space, "the great vibrating void," or "no-thing-ness."

McLaughlin aspired to make paintings that would function in the same way as the Karesansui garden at Ryõan-ji, rewarding the meditative observer with the epiphany that the garden and its 15 boulders were elegant pretexts for the contemplation of the space that separates them – what western art calls "negative space."

Tom Holste told me that McLaughlin, far from being a remote and glacial figure, was approachable and generous with his time, and that I should feel free to contact him. I did, but with some trepidation: I was an art student, and McLaughlin was an acknowledged master – to my mind, a superstar.

McLaughlin had never been overly concerned with the craft of painting and his tableaux often developed internal vices (the same could be said of Pollock). The small oil sketch I had was showing signs of wear and aging, if not actual damage, perhaps because of internal problems, no doubt exacerbated by transplanting from one place to another for years.

I telephoned him using the pretext of asking if he knew a

restorer that he could recommend. He told me that he would have to see the painting and invited me to bring it to him at his home.

When I arrived I was invited into his living room where his wife had prepared a tray of coffee and cakes; we spoke for nearly two hours before coming to the subject of my painting. Perhaps because of his patrician upbringing, and surely because of his age (he was 72), I had the impression that I was in the presence of an English gentleman of the old school. I asked him a myriad of questions about his relation to contemporary art. He answered intelligently and fulsomely, especially considering that he felt he had few peers or predecessors in western art. His intentions were so very different, he said, although he admitted to a kinship with Malevich whom he considered one of the few Western artists to share his concern with "pure" abstraction.

After a couple of hours the topic of my painting came up; he asked if I could leave it with him and he would study it…and to please call again in a week or so. I did, and once again I was invited to a coffee and a fascinating discussion of Zen (or Ch'an) Buddhist painting. He spoke of his admiration of the Southern Sung dynasty landscape painters, of their balance between the represented (form) and the void (the amorphous matrix of all form). He spoke respectfully of Mu-Qi's masterpiece, *Six Persimmons.* As our conversation drew to a close, McLaughlin brought up the question of my painting. He thought it impossible to restore so he was in the process of repainting it for me. I was astonished, and wasted not a minute telling my friend Tom, who was unsurprised: "I told you he was like that."

I made my third and last visit to McLaughlin a few weeks after that and once again we spoke at great length, this time asking after Bill Current and inquiring about my work. He was very kind but said that photography, with its unbreakable bond to representation, was an unsuitable medium to pursue pure abstraction. I didn't argue. He had repainted the painting for me, refusing any form of compensation; I took my painting, thanked him profusely, and left.

It never crossed my mind until much, much later that he was a bit lonely and more than tolerating my – and Tom's – intrusions, he welcomed them. Younger artists held him in such awe that they were intimidated by the idea of approaching him, and he spent most of his last years in seclusion with his wife.

McLaughlin's importance – his greatness – was an article of faith for my generation of California artists. He is arguably the first Los Angeles artist to transcend parochial and provincial interests, years before the Ferus Gallery opened and refocused the attention of the larger world on Southern California as an art center.

I found it a rude shock to see how under-appreciated and misunderstood his work was in New York – the *Welthauptstadt der Kunst* in the 60s and 70s. His work was woefully miscast as proto-Op-Art in the ill-conceived *Responsive Eye* exhibition organized by William Seitz at MoMA in 1965.

Even now the Wikipedia entries on McLaughlin show him as a Minimalist *avant le mot*; but, in fact, he never considered himself that. Nor is it surprising that the tough-art New York School of the 60s, with its doctrine of literalism ("what you see is what you see") dismissed any reference to Eastern philosophy as merely another instance of flaky West Coast mysticism. But if McLaughlin was no Minimalist, neither could he be comfortably placed in the company of artists like Mark Tobey or Morris Graves.

If McLaughlin's progenitors and contemporaries are rather thin on the ground, his inheritors are legion. Much of what came to be known as "California Light and Space" – artists such as Robert Irwin, James Turrell, Maria Nordman, Doug Wheeler, Larry Bell, John McCracken, Peter Alexander, and Craig Kauffman – are his direct descendants. Michael Asher's reductionist esthetic shows McLaughlin's influence, as do the works of painters as diverse as Don Dudley and David Reed. It is hardly stretching a point to say that the early paintings of Brice Marden and of Robert Ryman seem to indicate an awareness of McLaughlin.

McLaughlin's paintings are intelligent, refined and are intended to reward contemplative viewing. There is no compromise in his work; McLaughlin is the quintessential "difficult" artist. He was an artists' artist; no praise could be higher.

[1] *The Photographer and the American Landscape*, Museum of Modern Art, New York, September 24 – November 28, 1963. Catalogue. John Szarkowski's first exhibition as Director of the Department of Photography at MoMA.
[2] *Four Abstract Classicists,* curated by Jules Langsner, Los Angeles County Museum of Art. Catalogue. 1959 exhibition which included works by John McLaughlin, Lorser Feitelson, Karl Benjamin, and Frederick Hammersley.
[3] Bruce Nauman was living and working in the Bay Area at this time but was lying low. He spoke of San Francisco artists at that time as having a "hiding out" tradition. And, in 1969, he, too, moved to Los Angeles (from an interview with Willoughby Sharp, included in Janet Kraynak, ed., *Please Pay Attention, Please – Writing and Interviews,* (Cambridge: The MIT Press, 2003).
[4] It was an extremely interesting time to be at the Claremont Colleges – more interesting than I could have imagined before enrolling. The story of this period is well told in *It Happened at Pomona Art at the Edge of Los Angeles 1969–1973,* Rebecca G. McGrew, ed., 2011.

This text first appeared in the catalogue for the exhibition *John McLaughlin, Ed Ruscha, Lewis Baltz,* Galerie Thomas Zander, February 11 – April 29, 2012.

THE TEXTS BY LEWIS BALTZ WERE PREVIOUSLY PUBLISHED IN:

1. *Image* (the journal of the George Eastman House) Vol. 17, No.2 (June, 1974)
2. *Aperture*, No. 98 (Spring, 1985)
3. *The Times Literary Supplement*, London, 4 March 1994
4. *Art In America,* Vol. 63, No. 2 (March-April, 1975): 41-43.
5. Text originally appeared in *Landscape*: *Theory*, ed. Carol Di Grappa (New York: Lustrum Press, 1980) 23-39.
6. *American Images: Photography 1945–1980*, ed. Peter Turner (London: Barbican Art Gallery / Penguin Books, 1985)
7. *Camera Austria*, German trans. W. Prantner, No 26 (1988)
8. *The Deaths in Newport* [CD Rom] (Rotterdam: Paradox, 1995)
9. Delivered at the symposium *The Fault Zone*, organized by the Getty Center for the Humanities at the Los Angeles Municipal Art Gallery, Barnsdall Park, May 1992, on the occasion of Joe Deal's retrospective exhibition. Other panelists were Joe Deal, Kurt Forster, Frank Gehry, Marvin Heiferman, and Dennis Oppenheim.
10. *L'Architecture d'Aujourd'hui*, no. 300 (Sept. 1995).
11. "Sans-abri, sans lendemain," in *L'Architecture d'Aujourd'hui*, no. 303 (Sept. 1996)
12. "Jeff Wall, peintre de la vie moderne," in *L'Architecture d'Aujourd'hui*, no. 305 (June, 1996)
13. "Burden & Sekula, poissons et sous-marins," in *L'Architecture d'Aujourd'hui*, no. 312 (September 1997)
14. "Felix Gonzales-Torres, (sans titre)," in *L'Architecture d'Aujourd'hui*, no. 306 (September 1996).

15. *Absolute Landscape: Contemporary photography between illusion & reality* (Yokohama: Yokohama Museum of Art, 1997)
16. Previously unpublished, composed ca. 1997
17. Slavica Perkovic, *Vertigo* (Walther König, Cologne, 2012)
18. This text is a transcription from an audio installation in the exhibition *La Ville, Le Jardin, La Mémoire: 1999 La Mémoire*, Académie de France à Rome, Villa Medici, Rome, Italy, 1999, and features an audio interview with Michela Terreri who is the primary of the three co-authors of this piece, along with Slavica Perkovic and Lewis Baltz.
19. "Tosca" was written in 1999 and was all that I could salvage out of (what turned out to be an unnecessarily) frustrating period when I was briefly at the American Academy in Rome and was trying to secure authorizations to film on the sites of Tosca, nearly everybody's favorite opera.
20. "Notes sur Thomas Ruff," in *L'Architecture d'Aujourd'hui*, no. 313 (October 1997)
21. *Purple* No 5, Summer 2000
22. *Migropolis: Venice / Atlas of a Global Situation*, ed. Wolfgang Scheppe (Ostfildern: Hatje Cantz, 2010)
23. *Meetings with remarkable Men: John McLaughlin.* From the exhibition catalogue *John McLaughin, Ed Ruscha, Lewis Baltz,* Galerie Thomas Zander, Cologne, February 11 – April 29, 2012.

I want to heartily thank my readers, Marlene Klein, Chris Balaschak, Stefan Gronert, Matthew S. Witkovsky, and of course Michael Mack for their generosity, patience, and excellent advice.

Texts annotated by Chris Balaschak.

First edition published in 2012

Book design: Steidl Design
Production and printing: Steidl, Göttingen

Steidl / Düstere Str. 4 / 37073 Göttingen, Germany
Phone +49 551 49 60 60 / Fax +49 551 49 60 649
mail@steidl.de
www.steidlville.com / www.steidl.de
ISBN 978-3-86930-436-6
Printed in Germany by Steidl